M000012924

LIONS IN WAIT

a road to personal courage

by

Ragini Elizabeth Michaels

Facticity  Trainings

Seattle, Washington

Copyright ©1993 Ragini Elizabeth Michaels

All rights Reserved. This book or any part thereof may not be reproduced in any form whatsoever without written permission from the publisher.

Library of Congress Catalog Card Number: 92-91210

ISBN 0-9628686-1-2

Illustrations: Anugito Ten Voorde
Cover Design: Connolly Productions
Layout and Design: LaserWorl Inc.
Book Production: Patterson Printing

Published by:

Facticity Trainings, Inc.
Post Office Box 22814
Seattle, Washington 98122 U.S.A.
206-462-4369

to my father, who gave the
gift of calling me Ragini
before he died . . .

to my mother, whose
incredible love has remained
no matter what . . .

to Mary, Ben and Sue, whose
continuing acceptance and
support of me and all my
weirdness, says one hell of a
beautiful lot about them.

Acknowledgements

I'd like to thank Joseph Goldstein and Jack Kornfield for their beautiful introduction into my life of so many valuable old Buddhist metaphors, and my good friend Raga for his dedication to metaphorical storytelling and giving me the foundations I needed to story tell in my own way.

I'd like to acknowledge that so many of the truisms found in this book came into my awareness through my years with Osho. I also appreciate and acknowledge the influence of the metaphor work created by Dr. Milton H. Erickson, Steve and Carol Lankton, Connirae and Steve Andreas, Richard Bandler and John Grinder.

Thanks to Basira for her beautiful creative input, to Nadine, Rajanila, Suryo and Madita, for their care-filled editing and proofreading, and to Ambodha for his support, present in hundreds of small and essential ways.

Credit and thanks is extended to all who, like me, are in search of a better understanding of how to live in peace.

TABLE OF CONTENTS

Lions In Wait

Lions In Wait

Dear Reader . . .

Caution: Your Permission Is Requested!

This book will address your unconscious mind directly. Therefore, please be certain that you wish to begin re-educating that mind to relax with the flow of Opposites.

The benefits of *Lions In Wait* are best received when the book is read in a certain manner. Because the bulk of these chapters are trance-scripts, they are best enjoyed when read slowly, breathing in or pausing each time the eye sees the dots spaced between the words.

If you wish to receive maximum trance experience for yourself, read the words out loud, breathing in a rhythm with the spacing on the page, exhaling as you read the words, inhaling or pausing with each set of dots.

If you are familiar with the author's hypnosis tape series (*Remembrance* and *Facticity*), you can utilize their featured process of AAH (Acoustic Associative Hypnosis). Having heard the side of these tapes with voice and music, you have accustomed your unconscious mind to the sound and rhythm of the author's voice and associated those feelings with the music in the background.

If this is a pleasurable and positive association for you, you can now play the 'music only' side on the tapes as you read these chapters slowly. This will create maximum potential for the unconscious mind to use this type of trance experience, i.e., reading trance-scripts, in the most powerful manner by triggering already learned associations with the hypnotic process.

This Book . . .

includes trance-scripts of 10 trance experiences given spontaneously in 1987 to a small group of 20 people over 10 weeks of
time. Each person in the group considered themself to be a
spiritual seeker or someone in search of understanding, freedom, consciousness or love.

These trances were given in the spirit of exploration - the
exploration of a possible new way to accelerate the availability
and presence of consciousness and non-judgemental or choiceless awareness into everyday life.

These evenings were designed to re-educate the *unconscious*
process to the presence of Opposites as a facticity of life, and
to the creation of new ways of being with this pattern of
existence (duality) which would support, enrich and expand
our experience of living.

If you have tasted that place beyond the mind and body, and
would like to explore re-shaping the mind to befriend your
journey home, this book may be useful. It is based on evoking
unconscious memories of things you already know are true to
help you relax with the presence of duality and develop the
ability to trust your own previously discounted experience of
living.

These trance-scripts include certain words printed in bold type throughout. This is based on the Ericksonian Hypnotic technique of multiple level communication and sets up a pattern of communication with your unconscious mind directly even as your conscious mind reads the words.

Please be certain to awaken fully to the present time and space after completing each chapter. To help you return to a fully awake state, each chapter includes the following visual image to symbolize the message WAKE UP!

wake up!

Lions In Wait

A Note from Ragini . . .

Many of us have been living our lives as mice, disliking the feel of being so small. We have made many moves to change, to alter life styles and ourselves to evolve toward that seemingly ever elusive form of the Lion - King Of The Jungle - a single roar clearing the roads of any dangers, any difficulties, any pain - and paving the way for a journey of untold ease and comfort and freedom.

If you are also one of the people who have been working hard to convince the mouse that s/he really can roar - and you are ready to explore the probability that you have not been a mouse after all - but a lion in wait - this book is for you.

Lions In Wait

Prologue

Somehow she was always sitting when I arrived, her feet tucked up under the skirt, forever hanging gracefully and still. Her chin always seemed to rest between the forefinger and thumb of her hand. As I would watch her gazing out the window, I could feel the air pulsing with calm and silence. I would immediately begin to breathe more easily.

Some who met her seemed to see just another woman. But for me, the radiance emanating forth was unmistakable and indefineable. Annie had played the role of "my godmother" for years, yet I never really knew who she was, or why in her presence I always seemed to remember to feel good - especially about myself.

I'm not even certain anymore how she actually looked, but I know she was the most beautiful woman I've ever known. She could have become addictive so quenching was her presence - like drinking from a deep pool textured with refreshment unlike anything I had ever tasted before.

But addiction was never possible, for Annie always gave me back to myself. She led me on journey after journey through my own mind and soul, awakening something mysteriously beautiful within and nourishing a trust in simply being myself.

For some, it's the trees or the wind, some special place by the sea, or deep in the middle of a forest. For me, it was sitting there in that room, basking in the warmth of the smiles and the ease of the laughter - entranced by the wonderful wisdom of her words.

When she spoke, sound and silence partnered in an intriguing dance - motion and stillness playing a rhythm so stirring I could feel the wings of my Being readying to fly. I learned from Annie the presence of my spirit and its desire to soar and sing out the songs hidden so long in my heart.

I will share with you what I remember - and perhaps that silent song of your soul will also begin to sing.

Chapter 1

CHANGE - The Permanent Chameleon

The day's cyclone of change had left me filled with exhaustion and frustration. As I entered the room, I began to feel, as I usually did in her presence, a gentle breeze of quiet blowing by, soft and lazy. My body immediately began to respond to the soothing sensations of this space as Annie, perched by the window, seemed a perfect part of the early evening twilight melting before my eyes into the night.

I could feel tensions releasing even though my mind continued to hold my questions. What to do with this stream of constant change, always pressuring and cajoling me with its challenge to create that lasting feeling of success and completion? I knew without speaking Annie was aware of my tiredness and turmoil. I remember her speaking to my trembling and quaking soul, somehow knowing of its desire to find a way out of this game it was being forced to endure each day.

As I watched her beckon me forward, her hair catching and dancing with the last rays of the setting sun, I could feel my heart begin to lift as her beauty inspired me to drink deeply of the moment. She began, as she always did, my name on her lips sounding like a song.

*N*icholas, my friend,

   come and relax . . . listen for awhile . . .

   you can sit or change that position . . .

so comfort can come . . .

and you can, if you like . . .

relax those eyes . . . that forehead and jaw . . .

because I know you did come here now . . .

for something you want . . .

and perhaps your conscious mind has one idea . . .

and your unconscious mind has another about why it's here

and now . . .

and both of those minds can take as much as they'd like to

receive . . .

these words helping you to touch or see or **feel** . . .

what it is you came here to gather . . .

for **yourself** . . . right **now** . . .

*A*nd it's a curious thing how a person can forget to

   remember . . .

      you can **relax** with change. . . .

         for there are many places in life, aren't there? . . .

         where each person already knows how . . .

to relax with that flow . . .

and your conscious mind . . .

and your unconscious mind can . . .

listen *and hear what you need to hear . . .*

to go ahead now . . .

and begin to **allow** *this new step in your journey . . .*

beginning to take shape . . . to take form . . .

in a way just right for you . . . because after all . . .

there really is no way to travel your journey . . .

other than your way . . .

*A*nd your **unconscious mind** *can know . . .*

to **feel free** *. . . to take whatever it would like . . .*

and **use** *these* **learnings now** *. . .*

in the most **appropriate** *way for you . . .*

a traveler who's come here now . . .

for *that rest . . .*

that time to receive nourishment . . .

allowing a **deep relaxation** *to begin . . .*

continuing here and now . . .

allow*ing those deep mysteries . . .*

of that space **within** *. . .*

to work their wonders now . . .

in their own way . . .

*A*nd it's all right to listen with that conscious
mind as well . . .

or drift and dream a dream . . .

of how nice it can **feel** . . .

to be with **what is** . . .

the sounds . . . the feeling of the body where it **rests** . . .

the sensations of right now . . .

as you **allow** your **awareness** to flow with the changes . . .

of simply being here . . .

because you do know how, don't you? . . .

to **relax with change** . . .

and it's so easy at the right time . . .

to take off those clothes at night . . .

and just let them fall away . . .

stepping into that next place where you can rest **easily** . . .

and some people take off their clothes and drift **into** a

pleasant sleep . . .

allowing those clothes to just **rest** there on the floor . . .

while others hang those garments up neatly . . .

others climbing into yet another piece of **comfortable feeling**

cloth . . .

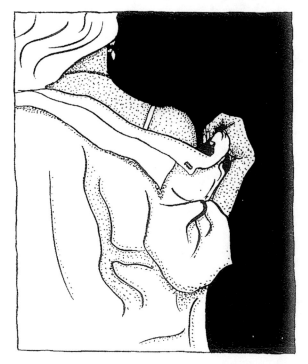

some people take off their clothes and drift into sleep...

they can stretch out in . . .

*and allow to encompass that **body** as it **relax**es . . .*

*A*nd most people **recognize** now . . .

that sleep at night is a cycle . . .

*through which a person can move **easily** . . .*

and with comfort . . .

*just as the seasons **change in** their **cycles** . . .*

a person learns to relax with the changes of the season . . .

haven't you? . . .

recognizi.g *the freshness of the spring as it springs forth . . .*

*from the bleak hardness of **the** winter's ground . . .*

*the freshness of the spring **flow**ing in its own way . . .*

easily and gently . . . on into the heat of the summer . . .

its own feelings hot and humid . . .

its own sights and sounds . . .

as it moves on its way toward that refreshing coolness of fall . . .

*A*nd without concern for whether they will be amber,

mauve or gold . . .

the leaves change . . .

***allow**ing the seasons to season that **life** . . .*

moving on to that time of rest . . .

those winter months when everything becomes still . . .

*the **move**ment becomes quiet . . . a **deep**ly . . . unseen . . .*

preparation for the spring . . .

already beginning . . .

even in the depths of the cold . . .

and when the time is right . . . the spring comes . . .

spilling forth on its own . . .

in its own time . . .

in its own way . . . fresh . . .

renewed by the shift of seasons that come and go . . .

changes emerging into spring . . .

begun long before the buds begin to blossom . . .

readying their fragrance to dissolve inside the wind . . .

nd as the seasons change . . .

the flora shifts . . .

the fauna adjusts . . .

animals and birds living in the north . . .

move toward the south when the winter comes . . .

toward that warmth . . .

***allow**ing the **change to come** . . .*

and with the seasons comes the change of that place to live . . .

and the changes flow . . .

in the south as well . . .

those animals and birds living in the south . . .

moving north as the seasons change . . .

*allowing a natural **trust** . . .*

*of that **inner knowing** can be followed . . .*

nd perhaps the birds become aware . . .

of their time to let go of those feathers . . .

feathers fully grown become dead . . .
*and **it's time to let go** . . .*
*and **allow the new** feathers to come forth . . .*
why many birds lose their feathers once a year . . .
and I wonder if that's a lot for a bird . . .
*to **be aware** of its need to let go when the time is right . . .*

And some birds let go of all their feathers . . .
> *at the same time . . .*
>> *remaining flightless for awhile . . .*
>>> *while others let go of just the feathers in the wing . . .*
and when the new ones grow in . . .
why the feathers on the body proper begin to fall away . . .
*and a bird could have many **feel**ings about those changes . . .*
*as it allows itself to trust **that deep inner knowing** . . .*
that the time for change is come . . .

And many animals in life . . .
***let go** of what might even be a second skin . . .*
*in order **to allow the new** one to come forth . . .*
and that might be a painful feeling for a snake . . .
*to **go ahead** at just the right time . . .*
and swell the veins on the top of its head . . .

following that **inner pull** to rub that head on a rock . . .

until that outer skin begins to crack . . .

freeing that snake . . .

to shed that entire outer skin all

at once . . .

to crawl on out and allow

the **new** skin **to**

emerge . . .

fresh and alive . . . with a new sense of being free . . .

to move with the new . . .

and allow that **old** . . . **can fall away** . . .

*Y*ou know . . .

there is no right way . . .

to let go of what's old . . .

because a snake does it one way . . .

a bird does it another . . .

and there's even still that lobster . . .

when **the time is** somehow **right** . . .

swallowing hugh amounts of that water to swell its body up . . .

creating such pressure on its shell . . .

that it begins to crack . . .

in its very weakest point . . .

causing that shell to begin to loosen . . .

and freeing the lobster to crawl away . . .

and that body immediately grows . . .

without a moments wait . . . to its new size . . .

and then the lobster rests . . .

allowing a new shell to be formed . . .

protection for its new journey . . .

as a larger, more expanded being . . .

ready to move back . . .

into the flowing waters once again . . .

*A nd even as the waters **move through change** . . .*

just as you can feel yourself changing . . .

*in those depths of **relaxation now** . . .*

*listening and **allow**ing . . . as you rest here . . .*

*changing with these words **that flow** like water can flow . . .*

in streams . . .

beginning with a trickle at the top of the mountain . . .

getting wider and deeper as it moves down and down . . .

from the tiny trickle . . .

*into a rushing stream flowing **smooth and easy** . . .*

or perhaps those choppy rapids . . .

stretching on out in their movement to return to the source . . .

and even as the stream becomes bigger and wider . . .

expanding . . . deepening . . .

the stillness does continue at the deepest depth . . .

even as the surface of the waters shift . . .

for the waters move . . .

to fill and create . . .

even those things that we've begun to think are here to stay . . .

the lakes . . . the ponds . . .

seemingly here forever . . .

yet but a temporary feature on the surface of this earth . . .

eventually disappearing . . .

why even that rushing force of water at Niagara Falls . . .

through that natural movement of erosion . . .

has made its way upstream . . .

many many miles from where it began . . .

like the body . . .

many miles from where it began . . .

continues to change . . .

even as you **rest** *here* **now** *. . .*

*T**he need to move . . .*

to be still . . .

the need to listen . . . the need to drift . . .

the changes that come and go . . .

and your unconscious mind can **become aware** *. . .*

of its **ability to relax with change** . . .

to know now . . .

change **is** as **natural** as that breath . . .

bringing in fresh oxygen now, isn't it? . . .

in exchange for that carbon dioxide . . .

going out with each exhalation . . .

the exchange is there . . .

to know . . .

you can **trust** . . . your **ability** . . .

to relax with this flow . . .

even as your unconscious mind . . .

begins to **remember you know** . . .

how to move with change . . .

*B*ecause after all, that body has changed from the time you
were a baby . . . into that toddler's body . . .
on up to that child's body . . .
that grew and **matur**ed during that
pubescent time . . .
into a teen body that has **ripen**ed . . .
into being that adult . . .
and with those changes come . . .
the changes in **those feelings** . . .
and how curious those feelings were, were they not? . . .

*when that body first **became aware** of those feelings . . .*

there in that private place . . .

new and unfamiliar feelings . . .

a change from the past . . .

*and **you've learned** about those changes now . . .*

and you've moved with many shifts . . .

changes of ideas and feelings . . .

places to live and people to love, haven't you? . . .

W*hile resting here . . .*

*as your unconscious mind **searches** there . . .*

to remember . . . your ability to relax . . .

*as you walk through **the days of your life** . . .*

the times of day change . . .

the temperatures change . . .

as the evenings come and go . . .

the phases of the moon change . . .

*and it's curious to **know** . . .*

*the new moon does its **change** where it cannot be seen . . .*

invisible while the night is dark . . .

*the new moon allows its change to **occur** . . .*

easily *. . .*

deep in the womb of the night . . .

*just as any of those old **limiting beliefs** . . .*

you know you're ready to let go of . . .

can begin to melt now . . .

there in the quiet privacy of the mind . . .

> * **loosening** their hold . . .*

>> *as you become aware . . .*

>>> *you can **relax** . . .*

>>>> *with change . . .*

*ou may not **be aware**, can you? . . .*

> *of those shifts already begun here . . .*

>> *changes that your unconscious mind has **allowed** . . .*

*in **the rhythm of** that breathing . . .*

*the pulse rate . . . **chang**ing that feeling . . .*

so you can rest . . .

and allow. . . that relaxation . . . .

continuing to come now . . .

*and **free** you to welcome . . .*

*with an **easy movement** . . .*

> *as easily **as you awaken** to the morning . . .*

>> *allowing the transition **from sleep** to come . . .*

>>> *in your own way . . . .*

in your own time . . .

and your unconscious mind can take these words . . .

and cause that conscious mind now and in the future . . .

to continue becoming aware . . .

*of **change** that **is natural** . . . to being alive . . .*

*to being **a part of existence** . . .*

that stretches and creates itself anew with each breath . . .

A̲nd just as you've allowed changes to occur . . .

opening that unconscious mind to receive what you came here

to gather . . .

that nourishment . . .

that support . . .

*changes you can **feel** continuing to happen now . . .*

***movement and** new **vision from a higher place** . . .*

and you deserve this time to rest, didn't you? . . .

to continue becoming aware now . . .

you really do have something you've been searching for . . .

throughout this journey . . .

and within that inner space . . .

*you can **rest** as **deeply** as you wish now . . .*

allowing your unconscious mind to begin to sort through its

*own **know**ings . . .*

*allowing a recognition of **how much** . . .*

***you already know** about relaxing with change . . .*

*I*sn't it curious that even a big heavy ship in the
sea . . .

might resist the directions to change direction . . .

and keep right on going . . .

maybe a mile or more the way it no longer needs to go . . .

even after that rudder goes down in the water . . .

and the new directions have been given . . .

yet a captain who knows his vessel . . .

allows that time . . .

to resist that **change of course** . . .

knowing full well that resistance allowed will reach its

completion . . .

the new direction eventually taking hold . . .

*A*nd that knowing . . .

can cause the unconscious mind now . . .

to locate those old beliefs you're ready to leave behind . . .

and **use your own experience** . . .

easily and more intensely now . . .

uncovering that new direction of your choice . . .

trusting that inner sense . . .

of your ability to **know** . . .

without a doubt . . .

*rests in that ability to trust . . . **that inner sense** . . .*

*L**ike the caterpillar . . .*

somehow allowing itself to follow that inner urge . . .

spinning a cocoon all around itself . . .

enveloping its very being in a protective darkness for awhile . . .

while a transformation can occur . . .

and that caterpillar doesn't realize, does he? . . .

that butterfly has always been there . . .

invisible and uncreated on the inside . . . yet present . . .

waiting for its time to emerge . . .

he simply trusts that inner pull to move in a certain direction . . .

to do certain things . . .

and allows each step of that journey to unfold . . .

*A**nd, yes . . .*

*the **unconscious mind** can spin its own cocoon . . .*

of comfort and ease now . . .

***develop**ing that ability . . .*

to be still and know . . .

the presence of yourself . . .

can feel that pull . . .

hear that small silent voice . . .

see that inner vision reflecting . . .

an image unknown to the eye of your mind . . .

*this **transformation** continuing at the right pace for you . . .*

allowing the unconscious mind that freedom . . .

to go ahead now . . .

*and **explore your experience** . . .*

can be a guide to guide you on your way . . .

to allowing that change . . .

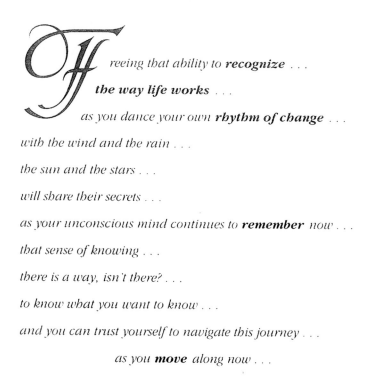

*reeing that ability to **recognize** . . .*

***the way life works** . . .*

*as you dance your own **rhythm of change** . . .*

with the wind and the rain . . .

the sun and the stars . . .

will share their secrets . . .

*as your unconscious mind continues to **remember** now . . .*

that sense of knowing . . .

there is a way, isn't there? . . .

to know what you want to know . . .

and you can trust yourself to navigate this journey . . .

*as you **move** along now . . .*

step by step . . .

*right to the **heart of the matter** . . . is within you . . .*

to trust . . .

to know . . .

to allow . . .

and invite your

unconscious

mind . . .

to explore those abilities to create . . .

a rhythm reflecting the dance of the winds . . .

a vision reflecting the beauty of the stars . . .

a feeling carrying you beyond the word . . .

   in your own way . . .

      because no matter what anyone has ever told you . . .

        *there is no way you can **be** anyone but **yourself** . . .*

          comfortably . . .

*That inner bridge being **creat**ed now . . .*

at the deepest levels . . .

will hand you the support, won't it? . . .

*and the **clarity** you need . . .*

to cross that bridge . . .

   from the land of belief into that realm of what is . . .

      your own life to live . . .

fully . . . freely . . .

in your way . . .

and just as

a child

doesn't

really know

how helpful

those feet

are going

to be . . .

walking that bridge some day . . .

when they're seen there for the first time before the eyes . . .

toes wiggling . . .

wondering what they are for . . .

> *those feet **learn**, didn't they? . . .*

> > *how to carry the body to places beyond the mind's eye . . .*

> > *and you may have forgotten the difficulties*

> > ***experienced** . . .*

when you first learned to stand . . .

on your own two feet for the very first time . . .

the challenge of letting go of that hand . . .

or perhaps it was the leg of the chair . . .

> > *or a rung on the side of that crib . . .*

yet whatever way you went through that learning . . .

you did learn, did you not? . . .

   to stand on your own . . .

*P*erhaps you're not aware . . .

that your unconscious mind . . .

went on to use that learning . . .

to help you not only stand . . .

but walk . . .

carrying you from one place to another . . .

***developing** that **ability** . . .*

into running and hopping and skipping . . .

and maybe even a jump or two . . .

*all abilities developed from that first step **of learning** . . .*

***you can** stand on your own two feet . . .*

and trust your own experience . . .

*P*erhaps you don't even think about it now . . .

you just stand on your own . . .

and trust that unconscious mind and body . . .

to continue using that learning . . .

*freeing you to **move gracefully** . . .*

   ***easily with** whatever **change** of posture comes . . .*

*A*nd *your unconscious mind can, isn't it? . . .*

using that same learning ability now . . .

stretching those abilities . . . to create new ways . . .

to carry you across that bridge to where you want to be . . .

yourself comfortably . . .

learning your way . . .

to dance with life . . .

is a way . . . to enjoy . . .

and you can know your unconscious mind . . .

will continue this work . . .

that you've requested continuing now . . .

*allowing that mind to **learn from** that vast wealth . . .*

*of previously **discounted experience** . . .*

***that is yours** . . .*

*T*rusting *. . . your ability . . . to just be . . .*

who you are . . .

can begin to unfold . . . even more deeply . . .

*to hand you that **freedom** . . .*

***to relax with that permanent flow of change** . . .*

A nd in a few moments . . .

just as you have learned, haven't you? . . .

to awaken in the morning . . .

from a deeply refreshing sleep . . .

you can begin to feel an energy returning . . .

your awareness more and more inside that body now . . .

resting there in that very supportive place . . .

allowing those energies . . .

continue returning . . .

re-energizing . . .

knowing this work will continue . . .

in ways that will be most appropriate for you . . .

*can **allow** yourself that next step now . . .*

yours to take . . .

as you bring yourself . . .

more and more toward right here and now . . .

coming all the way to the present as you begin to feel that

***awareness** . . .*

*returning you to **this time and this place** . . .*

resting right here and right now . . .

taking your time . . .

as you allow yourself . . .

*to move easily toward that refreshed **awake**ned state . . .*

feeling a deepening sense of knowing . . .

your unconscious mind can learn from your own experience . . .

*and **awaken** more and more easily now . . .*

*stretching all the way into the present and **be**ing **fully** right*

***here**.*

wake up!

THOUGHTS:

Chapter 2

DANCING WITH OPPOSITES -
The Circle Of Completion

Confusion and distress filled my mind and body as I entered her room. A dark cloud of questions hung over me, enveloping like a heavy blanket of suffocation. Why is there no end to this quest for love and comfort? What am I doing wrong to keep the darker side of my nature continuing to emerge again and again? Why is there still so much greed and lust and pain in my heart?

I managed to lift the veil of confusions and despair just enough to become aware of Annie, sitting as always, seemingly undisturbed. I noticed a shadow draped across her shoulder, falling with a menacing sharpness onto the soft curves of her lap. I wondered how this darkness dared to move in her presence, when the light of her Being shown so bright.

As always, Annie sensed my state of mind, and before I knew it, she was speaking to my deepest Being of things I'd forgotten I knew, and beckoning me to remember and relax.

*N*icholas, my friend,

just let your body find a comfortable position . . .

for after all . . .

comfort and the desire to **be comfortable** . . .

is one thing that makes people go places . . .

and you can go to just that depth of **relax**ation . . .

that will be the right depth for you . . .

to **allow** these **new learnings** . . .

these new expansions . . .

to **begin** to happen for you now . . .

even more easily . . .

*B*ecause you are a traveler, aren't you? . . .

someone who's been journeying a long time now . . .

and you may be here for many reasons . . .

and whatever those conscious reasons might be . . .

your **unconscious mind** can **use this time** . . .

to go ahead and gather for you . . .

what you came here to receive . . .

from those deeply . . .

mysterious levels of your being . . .

yourself . . .

F or every traveler knows . . .

energies comes when a traveler is traveling . . .

and sometimes those energies come in a burst . . .

much movement occurring very quickly, very fast . . .

while other times the energies run low . . .

the traveler knowing the time has come . . .

*to **move to** a **comfort**able place . . .*

*and **allow** a **rest** . . .*

can begin to occur . . .

like the night that comes . . .

softly enveloping that sleeper . . .

with a quiet yet vibrant sound . . . all around . . .

and those sounds can help that rest deepen . . .

allowing . . . a refreshing time to begin . . .

*because **this time** now . . .*

is your time . . .

*to allow your **unconscious mind** . . .*

to go ahead now . . . and remember . . .

***sort out** all those **experiences** that are yours . . .*

*of **how two things** that seem so **opposed** . . .*

*can actually **work together** . . .*

because there was a time . . .

when you were unaware, wasn't there? . . .

of the fact . . .

that those two feet . . .

being seen for the first time right out there in front of you . . .

*were somehow going to **learn** . . .*

to work together . . .

And although there might have been many times . . .

when that little body . . .

fell down . . .

crashed right on down to the earth . . .

or maybe it was that concrete so hard and cold . . .

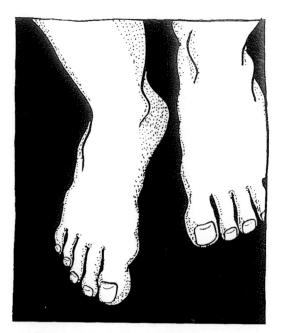

you have those two feet... and they can work together...

*Y*et it was that unpleasant learning how it feels to fall

down . . . that allowed your **unconscious mind** . . .

to be free now . . .

to **use that experience** . . .

of learning the feel of falling down . . .

to help you stand up . . .

and be free to walk . . . and run . . . and move . . .

beyond that old learning . . .

of how to lose your balance . . .

as you remember now . . .

that learning was essential, wasn't it? . . .

to **recogniz**ing and **develop**ing that ability to stand up . . .

on those two feet . . .

*O*f course sometimes . . .

a person gets an **idea** . . .

that there are things in life that are right . . .

and of course you do have a right foot . . .

yet the **opposite** of right is not always wrong, is it? . . .

because the foot that's left . . .

when you claim that right foot as the right one . . .

is the left foot that is left, isn't it? . . .

and if what's right is on the right . . .

and what's left somehow becomes wrong . . .

why it might be very hard . . .

to use that right foot alone because after **all** . . .

if that left foot is left behind . . .

well it's a little hard to **balance** on one foot . . .

and with that left left behind . . .

a person with only a **right** foot has to hop or jump, don't they? . . .

and make their way in a most cumbersome manner . . .

*A*nd it's nice to realize . . .

you have those two feet . . .

and they **can work together** . . . creating a partnership . . .

a circle of completion that carries you . . .

to that freedom . . . to move yourself . . .

in your own way now . . .

*Y*our **unconscious mind** . . .

   can take these words . . .

   and yes, **make maximum meaning** . . .

in a way that will be **most useful to you** . . .

for although that conscious mind operates on a

certain surface . . .

behind every surface there is a depth . . .

and that depth of your unconscious mind . . .

can continue taking these words now . . .

   and **re-collect** *for you . . .*

     all those **experiences** . . .

     that you've been gathering on your own . . .

       of how **two things seemingly opposed** . . .

       can **work together** . . .

Why even the pendulum on an old clock . . .

knows as it swings . . .

way over to that one side . . .

moving and gathering that momentum as it swings . . .

the pendulum will use that momentum . . . won't it? . . .

the moment it reaches that extreme . . .

to let go . . . and move easily to that other side . . .

*A*nd even as the energy dissipates . . .

that was gathered to carry that motion back . . .

to the other side . . .

a new energy is gathering . . .

that will carry that pendulum back yet again . . .

allowing the swing toward completion . . .

to continue moving . . .

dancing its dance . . .

like the tides rolling in . . .

rolling out . . .

a cycle . . .

where the one side depends on the other . . .

allowing its existence to rest poised . . .

in the womb of what is . . .

the opposite begins to take shape . . .

and although . . . there are many days . . .

when it seems like night will never come . . .

the cycle goes on . . .

the circle . . . completing itself . . .

allowing . . .

the **movement** . . .

like a bird balancing on a limb . . .

...the pendulum reaches that extreme... to let go to that other side..

__allow__s the movement from the wind . . .

delighting in its __freedom__ to hold onto that limb . . .

maintaining its place . . .

yet free __to let go__ . . .

and flow with that branch . . .

holding on as it rests there . . .

allowing the wind to move that branch . . .

in its own way . . .

nd what a delight for a bird to begin to

*know . . . its **ability** . . .*

to hold on while letting go . . .

to let go . . . while holding on . . .

*to that ability **to allow** . . .*

*the **remembrance** of those childhood plays . . .*

in that playground of see-saws and teeter-totters . . .

delighting in the exhilaration of moving up . . .

wondering at the pain of plopping down . . .

perhaps too hard on the ground . . .

*and how long does it take a child to **learn** . . .*

*of that **place in the center** of that see-saw . . .*

going back and forth . . .

*to **see what you saw** then . . .*

*can free you to see now **in a new way** . . .*

*And that **center** point . . .*

***remains unaffected** . . .*

***by** the change of that board, doesn't it? . . .*

*going **up** on one end . . .*

*while the other plops **down** . . .*

*using the momentum of that **natural flow** . . .*

*to change and **allow** . . .*

that circle of completion to come . . .

*A*nd a child standing in the **middle** of the see-saw game . . .

can hold onto that place . . .

that **position** right there in the center . . .

while letting go . . .

and allowing that body to **move** . . .

with the **natural** flow of **up** . . .

and **down** . . .

easily . . .

*W*hy even the muscles in the body know . . .

to allow movement to occur . . .

some muscles must contract and hold

on . . . while others . . . let go . . .

and relax . . . freeing the movement can

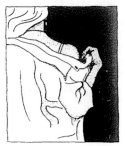

occur . . . and even that brain . . .

that allows the movement to happen so

naturally . . . has its own two sides . . .

connected by a middle . . .

each side playing its own role . . .

each needed to allow . . .

the circle to be complete . . .

and although a child **learns many things** . . .

it might be many years before a person remembers . . .

without the darkness of that chalkboard . . .

whether it be black or green . . .

why the white letters would never be seen . . . could they? . . .

they'd disappear and remain unknown . . .

just like the roots . . .

of something so beautiful as a water lily or a lotus flower . . .

allowing itself to open its petals to the sun . . .

sharing its fragrance . . .

with the wind . . .

W_{hy} that flower's roots . . .

deep down in the slimy mud . . .

are needed . . .

to allow that beautiful blossom to arise . . .

lifting itself right on up and out . . .

of that slimy, ooozy, gooey mud . . .

to be the beautiful blossom it is . . .

of course, a child knows how to enjoy . . .

playing in an oozy, gooey, slimy feeling . . .

enjoying how it feels to play with those feelings . .

*as you **remember what you need to know** now . . .*

*to allow . . . these **new abilities** . . .*

to begin . . .

and your unconscious mind can . . .

take these remembrances now . . .

as a traveler journeyed to many a peak . . .

and perhaps enjoyment resting in many a valley . . .

*and **you can know** . . .*

without those mountain peaks . . .

there can be no valleys . . . can there? . . .

*and **without those** valleys . . . why . . .*

there can be no mountain peaks . . .

and together . . .

*the terrain becomes **fresh** . . .*

*alive with **new** kinds of **life** . . .*

at every stage of the journey . . .

climbing up that mountain . . .

or climbing down into that valley . . .

*A*nd no matter what kind of ladder a person might use to climb . . .

well, without those bottom rungs . . .

*the higher points of view cannot be **reached** . . .*

they might look good up there . . .

*and you know they could get you **where you want to go** . . .*

but without the bottom . . .

the top remains distant . . . doesn't it? . . .

like the roots of the tree . . .

*the **deeper** they go . . .*

the more free is that tree . . .

to expand . . . or stretch tall . . .

to reach its way toward those stars . . .

twinkling in the night . . .

and without that night sky . . .

can the stars even be seen? . . .

for they remain there during the day . . .

invisible to the eye . . .

and only when that dark velvet backdrop falls . . .

the delight of the stars sparkle begins to show . . .

*N̸ow your **unconscious mind** may know . . .*

many of those old beliefs . . .

you've been given about those unpleasant feelings . . .

those things you were taught not to know . . .

that you were told go bump in the night . . .

and hang out with those ghosties and gouleys and goblins . . .

may be resting there . . . like the night skies . . .

to allow a new reflection to begin . . .

a light twinkling . . .

to show you something . . .

you were taught not to know . . .

and your unconscious-mind . . .

can take these words . . .

*and **allow your learnings** . . .*

*that you know . . . **in** your **experience** . . .*

how one kind of energy flows . . .

into the shape . . .

of what appears to be an opposing shape . . .

seemingly in opposition . . .

yet a harmony hidden there . . .

your knowing can continue arising now . . .

that every beginning is followed by an end . . .

which has within it, doesn't it now? . . .

an unseen beginning . . . a new beginning to begin . . .

*A*nd *these knowings . . .*

your unconscious mind can . . .

***continue to use your knowings** now . . .*

***trust**ing . . . that inner sense . . .*

you can allow your energies to flow . . .

***naturally** . . .*

like the waters of a river . . .

flow from the left bank to the right . . .

without concern . . .

*allowing that **flow** . . .*

*from **one side to the other** . . .*

as the river bed carries the water . . .

on its way . . .

continuing its journey . . .

of returning to that source . . .

your unconscious mind does knows . . .

*what brought you here to **listen** and rest . . .*

*and your **unconscious mind** has allowed this time . . .*

to be a time for that unconscious mind . . .

*to **create the space** . . .*

to allow those old beliefs . . .

*you are beginning to **sense now,** aren't you? . . .*

in your own experience . . .

*are **beliefs** you're **ready now** . . .*

*to **let go** of . . .*

*and **allow** . . . your **experience** . . .*

to become the basis . . .

*of a **freedom** . . . **to move** . . .*

with change . . .

that's right, to simply stretch out . . . now . . .

and allow . . . the energies of life . . .

to flow . . . from one place . . .

to another . . .

***allow**ing . . . that **flow** . . .*

from light . . .

***into dark**ness . . .*

***trust**ing . . . the **light rests** . . .*

***within** the deep womb of night . . .*

and will shine again . . .

dawning in its own brilliant creation . . .

as it spreads itself across the morning sky . . .

*F*or your unconscious mind can . . .

***learn** . . .**from** your experience . . .*

of the trees . . .

of the wind . . .

***your experience** of that sky . . .*

that remains boundless . . .

expansive behind the clouds . . .

allowing . . .

your experience of just how does nature . . .

invite the cold of winter . . .

so bleak and freezing . . .

to make that change . . .

into the hot, warm, summer sun . . .

and even though a person . . .

may not consciously be aware of that summer sun . . .

holding within it the seeds of winter's

discontent . . .

your unconscious mind knows, does it

not? . . .

*the **darkness follows the light** . . .*

*just as the **light follows the darkness** . .*

the ways of change flow . . .

Ａnd your unconscious mind can . . .

take those learnings now . . .

and clear a space . . .

*to **explore** new ways with ease . . .*

yes . . .

an easy letting go . . .

to explore that unlearning now . . . and allow . . .

your experience to fly free . . . to hand you a taste . . .

*of a new height . . . a **new perspective** . . .*

as radically different . . .

as the sky must seem to the butterfly . . .

so long encased in that tiny caterpillar world . . .

forced to stay grounded . . .

he unconscious mind can . . .

draw on that wonder of life . . .

even on down . . .

to the very cells of that body . . .

in which you're resting now . . .

comfortably unlearning . . .

freeing yourself . . .

*to **know** what you were taught not to know . . .*

yourself . . .

*and that **ability** . . . **to flow** . . .*

from the highest peak . . .

*brilliant **with the light** of the new height . . .*

to which you've flown . . .

*sliding with ease and comfort right on **in** . . .*

***to** even the **darkest**, deepest valley . . .*

knowing . . .

the valleys need the mountains to be, don't they? . . .

*the mountains resting **in the hands of** the valleys . . .*

and together . . .

the land becomes rich . . .

to travel . . .

and the very cells of that body traveling even now . . .

toward remembering . . .

that wealth of knowing *that is yours . . .*

the very cells of that body . . .

holding together now by the wondrous pull . . .

*between that **positive and** that **negative** force . . .*

resting naturally there inside those cells . . .

*A*nd *it is that very pull . . .*

between those seeming opposites . . .

*that **very natural connection** . . .*

between the positive and the negative . . .

that allows those cells to stay together . . .

freeing that body . . .

to move . . .

to be all that it can be . . .

and that's right . . . at the heart of the matter . . . isn't it? . . .

for the opposite of right . . .

isn't always wrong, is it? . . .

because what's left to do now . . .

*is **go ahead** and **learn** from that body's **wisdom** . . .*

that knows the beauty . . .

*the power **of allowing** . . .*

*that **positive and** that **negative** . . .*

do flow together . . .

to work together . . .

to explore that ability . . .

to say yes . . . to both . . .

f course even a simple thing like that hand . . .

yourself a new **grasp** *. . .*

on **how it feels to flow** *with that energy . . .*

from light to dark . . .

from up to down . . .

from in to out . . .

enjoying *the dance . . .*

that hands you that freedom to move . . .

just as the hand can be free to open . . . can't it? . . .

reaching out to receive . . .

within it the need to close . . .

rests waiting to arise . . .

to grasp and hold what is needed in yet another way . . .

and your **unconscious mind** *can fly free now . . .*

with these **remember**ings *. . . of all you were taught not to*

know . . . yourself . . . comfortably . . .

moving with the change of that energy . . .

and allowing . . .

Because **no matter how long it takes** . . .

a plant to bloom . . .

each blooms in its own time . . .

and some require just the right proportion of that light

and that dark . . .

like the Christmas cactus . . .

celebrates its blooming . . .

only when the light and the dark are balanced . . .

and then that Christmas Cactus explodes . . .

its unique beauty bursting forth . . .

and your unconscious mind can . . .

go ahead now . . .

and allow that conscious mind can now **be more aware** . . .

of those gifts . . .

life gives in the present . . .

that can be opened . . . and explored . . .

seen with a fresh eye . . .

heard with a clear ear . . .

felt with a new depth of feeling . . .

to receive those gifts . . .

the wisdom of existence itself . . .

handing you that wealth . . .

of your discounted experience . . . **is yours** . . .

to begin to draw upon now . . .

*S*o go ahead and **build** . . .

that **new, solid, yet flexible** . . .

unconscious foundation . . .

that can help you . . .

to keep your finger right on the flow of things . . . aren't you? . . .

be in touch . . .

with how life . . . expresses itself naturally . . .

you can learn . . . in your own way . . .

in your own time . . .

you can trust . . . your experience . . .

and allow . . . that's right . . . yourself now . . .

to continue trusting that unconscious mind . . .

will continue this work . . .

in just the right way for you . . .

*B*ecause some things you thought you could never do . . .

can happen, can't they? . . .

in ways you might never have known . . .

it's possible to move in a whole new way . . .

with a lightness that can even feel like soaring. . . .

allowing the rainbow of your feelings free . . .

to show their colors . . . and dance their heart . . .

blossoming in just your way . . .

Within every seed . . .

the blossom rests hidden . . . doesn't it? . . .

unmanifest . . . invisible to the eye . . .

*and you can know **in every** . . .*

*   **experience** . . .*

*   rests the seed . . .*

*   of its other side . . .*

*   and with that **knowing** . . .*

*   **you can** begin . . . to relax. . . .*

*   and **trust your abilities** . . .*

to move with life . . .

to flow like the river's water . . .

back and forth . . . up and down . . . in and round . . .

all that comes in its way . . .

***continuing** now on your journey . . .*

*to that source . . . of **being** . . .*

yourself . . .

comfortably . . .

And I'd like to invite your unconscious mind . . .

to go ahead and continue these new abilities . . .

*to **create new behaviors** . . .*

*   that can free you . . .*

*to **relax with change** . . .*

*to **dance with** the expressions of life . . .*

rising again and again through the flow of seeming

***opposites** . . .*

allowing the circles to complete . . .

relaxing in the beginning of the end . . .

and the end of each beginning . . .

*is yours to **feel** . . .*

to know . . . to allow . . .

***yourself** to begin now . . .*

***becoming aware** of that movement again . . .*

returning toward a time that's here and now . . .

Allowing your awareness of all that's around to

*begin **expand**ing . . .*

*and you can, if you like, take **that awareness** with you . . .*

wherever you go . . .

*and you can **gently** now become aware of a pull to come to*

an opposite place . . .

a place that instead of being deep inside . . .

is right out here . . .

*coming to a place where that **attention** moves . . .*

*from being in there to **out here** in this time and space . . .*

allowing your energies to begin to follow that pull

to move now in yet another direction . . .

***F**eel*ing the **energies** begin to manifest
that are pulling you toward here . . .

just like the pendulum of that clock carries itself toward
one side . . .

and then **uses** the **energy** that's been gathered . . .

to return to where it was before it began . . .

*A*nd yet some time has passed, hasn't it? . . .

and something happened that might be of importance to you . . .

and just allow yourself to feel the energies coming back into
the body **now** . . .

knowing your unconscious mind will continue this work

even when you sleep at night . . .

and of course . . .

at a deep enough level so you will sleep peacefully . . .

restfully . . .

and **wake up** in the morning . . .

feeling rested . . .

relaxed, **refreshed** . . .

stretching then as you can stretch now

as you like . . .

causing you to **come now** *. . .*

all the way **to** *this* **present**

and be **right here**, *fully wide awake and alert*

and continuing to **awaken** *as you move that body*

and come fully to this place

right here and right **now**.

wake up!

Chapter 3

STEPPING THROUGH THE SHADOWS — Death, Pressure & Pain

As I stood watching, I could feel my distress with the day's darkness as it covered the beauty of fall dissolving into winter. I was anxious with the growing awareness of my own body getting older, my hair greyer, and the pressures and pains of life more difficult to bear. I had read much about death and dying, but the thought of my life coming to an end as the fall was doing now, left me frightened and cold. I knew no-where to turn but to Annie.

As I entered my favorite place of sanctuary, I saw her simply sitting, without movement, yet alive with a vibrancy beyond words. Her head turned as she became aware of my presence. The grace with which the movement unfolded astonished my mind into silence. I noticed her hair was also more grey, and remembered she often spoke of her body as being in pain. I wondered how she could rest so deeply with death simply awaiting its time to claim her beauty and turn it to decay.

When she motioned me to sit, I could almost feel a breeze of comfort surround me. I knew there was something to understand about these shadows of life, but I hadn't any idea where to begin. Somehow, Annie always knew. Even without my speaking, she would guide me to the source of my questions and my answers - deep within. I began to soften as she whispered my name once again into the stillness of the shadows gently falling.

*N*icholas, my friend,

you can **remember** now how it feels to **relax** . . .

in a very **comfortable place** . . .

finding that most comfortable position . . .

*and just **allowing** the sounds . . .*

*and the sensations of now . . . as you **rest here** . . .*

*beginning to **receive the support** . . .*

*of what your **body** is **rest**ing upon . . .*

that body that's been with you for a long time now,

hasn't it? . . .

beginning a long time ago . . . as a single cell . . .

*W*ith the birth of that cell . . .

began the growth of that body. . . .

continuing to develop . . .

changing form and changing shape . . .

as it moves through time . . . toward becoming . . .

the body that is your body now . . .

*and there came that time . . . all **safe and warm** . . .*

protected there in that womb . . .

*where life was such a **comfortable feeling** . . .*

*perhaps the first **taste** of death began . . .*

when from your mother's side . . .

life emerged . . .

and your body entered this world . . .

and to many a child, perhaps that birth . . .

was a death of sorts . . .

*an ending of that **comfortable place** . . .*

and a beginning of this journey . . .

in your way now . . .

for that body has come here . . .

*to this **resting place** . . .*

journeying through its many sizes and shapes . . .

through many fashions and styles . . .

to bring you here . . . now . . .

*y̵our **unconscious mind** . . . can **listen** . . .*
  and feel free . . .

  *to take **these words that are being heard** . . .*

*and **use them** now . . .*

*in the most **appropriate way** . . .*

*to **continue** freeing you to **let go** . . .*

***of those old beliefs** . . . you're ready to set aside . . .*

*and **sort thru your experiences** now . . .*

  *to **grasp** yet a **newer vision** . . .*

causing you to **tune in** to the **harmony** . . .

hidden in that **changing of forms** . . .

occurring throughout life . . .

*F*or with every death . . .

does come a birth . . .

like that body . . . dying to its form as a baby . . .

taking birth as that toddler's body . . .

moving on to yet another **loss** . . .

of that baby tooth . . .

which every child knows . . .

signifies the beginning of the end . . .

of being that child . . .

readying itself to step forth . . .

and create the space for that adult tooth to arise . . .

long before the rest of the body . . .

becomes that adult body fully . . .

something deep inside that child knows . . .

it's time to end . . .

and allow the **new beginning to begin** . . .

ust as something deep within . . .

a seed planted in the earth . . .

knows . . . there will come a time . . .

when its casing must crack . . .

and it will die to being that seed . . .

freeing itself . . .

to take the shape of a seedling . . .

*free now . . . to **continue** on . . .*

*the **next stage** of that journey . . .*

emerging . . .

and a seed might have many feelings . . .

letting go of all that it's ever known . . .

and yet . . .

when the time comes for that

casing to crack . . .

*the **energy** of that seed bursts*

forth, does it not? . . .

***claiming** its **new shape** unfolding . . .*

allowing . . . the journey . . .

to go on . . .

***D**eep within* that soil . . .

***rest**s many organisms* . . .

*little micro-organisms that even the eye can't **see*** . . .

allowing what has decayed there . . .

*dead plant **life*** . . .

*the **death** of animal life* . . .

becoming a nourishment . . .

***reach**ing the **root**s of those little plants* . . .

and it's curious to recognize . . .

*a gardener's **understanding** knows* . . .

the more death you allow in your garden . . .

why the more life you'll have blossoming there . . .

*and that's a nice knowing to **know*** . . .

life** itself . . . **allows that end . . .

to always take the shape of a new beginning . . .

*W**hy even in the thickest bog* . . .

layers upon layers of death . . .

*decaying plant and animal life **sink deep*** . . .

packing themselves into one another . . .

and the time comes when that bog . . .

the peat growing deep . . .

changes . . . and becomes coal . . .

*from the **death** of all that lived in that bog . . .*

arises those black diamonds . . .

*a treasure that **brings** warmth . . .*

freeing the heat of fire to reach out . . .

melting the coldness of the dark . . .

*allowing **life** to emerge **again** . . .*

burning with its freedom to be . . .

like the embers of a fire . . .

when it appears as if the fire has died . . .

gone out and is no more . . .

why, those embers can burn for a long time, haven't they? . . .

ready to burst forth again with a flame . . .

allowing the light . . . to shine . . .

*A*nd does the flame of a candle . . .

remain the same flame that began the light beginning . . .

or does the flame change . . .

flickering into existence and flickering out of existence . . .

evaporating wispy in the air . . .

up . . . in . . . smoke . . .

and yet the flame burns . . . and the light shines

*A*s the light of the day . . .

    shines less and less as night begins to arrive. . .

surrounding quietly . . . the demise of day. . . .

the birth of the twilight begins . . .

and the end of each day . . .

brings the birth of the night . . .

and with the death of the night . . .

  comes the birth of the day . . .

    dawning . . .

      as it stretches itself across the sky . . .

        spilling into being like the spring springs forth . . .

          for there is no season more filled with pressure . . .

than the spring . . . the earth bulging . . .

seeds readying themselves to come forth . . .

pushing and pressing their way upward . . .

upward to leave the dark and come into the light . . .

and without that winter . . .

when **everything dies** *. . .* **to what it once was** *. . .*

creating that re-nourishment of the soil . . .

to be free to feed those seeds when the springtime comes . . .

why it's nice to know . . .

*out of winter's **death** . . .*

*does come the **birth** of spring . . .*

again . . . and again . . . and again . . .

Many people find . . . the end . . .

*is free to be the **end** . . .*

when the end is allowed to be the end . . .

*every end . . . **beginning** a new beginning . . .*

*and **the cycle goes on** . . .*

allowing . . .

*what was **once dead** . . .*

to take new form again . . .

*inviting **energies** to **transform** . . .*

*becoming **alive again** . . .*

to yet another shape . . . another style . . .

*Just as you have **changed**, have you not? . . .*

yet perhaps not aware that you have died . . .

to who you used to be . . .

when you were just those 12 years of age . . .

perhaps even said goodbye now to the you . . .

that was 21 . . .

and where did that you go . . .

as you are here? . . .

Y et the you of then . . .

was there then and gone now . . .

and you are here . . .

in yet another form . . . yet another shape . . .

yet another you . . . continuing . . .

to learn . . . **you can die to the moment** *. . .*

and be born to the next . . .

fresh and new . . .

as the cycle goes on . . . and on . . . and on . . .

and your unconscious mind . . .

can take these **learnings now** *. . .*

that are your learnings . . .

those **knowings that are your knowings** *now . . .*

and continue to go ahead . . .

build that solid, yet flexible unconscious foundation, won't

you? . . .

that can free you . . .

*to **step** more easily now **through those shadows** . . .*

of death, pressure and pain . . .

for where there is an object in the light . . .

a shadow is cast, is it not? . . .

and did you know . . .

the brighter the light . . .

the darker the shadow? . . .

*and isn't it curious to **recognize** . . .*

> *a **shadow has no substance of its own** . . .*
>
> *yet is an experience to experience . . .*
>
> *your experience more **comfortably now** . . .*

And your unconscious mind can go on . . .

sort *through **those experiences** now and in the future. . .*

*and **create** for you that **new perspective** . . . that new*

***feel**ing . . .*

*that new sense of **harmony** . . .*

with *the **experience of dying** to what is done . . .*

becoming free . . .

to step fully alive . . .

into that gift of now . . . that present always here . . .

for you . . . as your very own . . .

*J*ust how **free** can it be . . .

to let go . . .

of those **old beliefs** and ideas . . .

continuing **to fall away now** . . .

as you continue to **trust your own experience** . . .

allowing your unconscious mind . . .

use that **experience** now . . . **to guide you** on your way? . . .

*A*nd as the darkness of those shadows
beginning to fade . . .

the light of your own **understandings** continuing

to **dawn** . . . like a new **awaken**ing day . . .

you can feel **free to relax** . . .

allowing your unconscious mind . . .

to make maximum use yet again . . .

of all these words . . . in a manner most appropriate to

you . . .

because after all . . .

everyone who's a human being . . .

knows the experience of pain . . . don't you? . . .

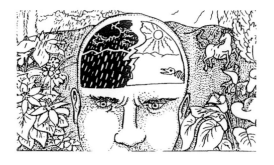

yet people are taught . . . not to know . . .

many things about pain . . .

and yet that experience . . . of those sensations in the body . . .

perhaps sharp . . . dull . . . tingling . . . numb . . .

perhaps cold or fire-hot . . .

*are sensations a person can **watch** . . .**with wonder** . . .*

as those sensations move and change . . .

*that experience people call **pain** . . .*

*that **indicator** . . . the **body wants your attention** . . .*

and the body has its own way of communicating to that

conscious mind . . .

*that it's time now for you to go and **do** . . .*

***what you need** to do . . .*

to take care of yourself . . .

allowing the sounds of those inner voices from the past . . .

to be set aside . . .

as you can take care of the body now . . .

*L*ike the body . . . the heart . . .

has its own kind of pain . . . doesn't it? . . .

perhaps alerting you . . .

the rhythm of your movement is out of step . . .

with the dance of being yourself . . .

and the wisdom of your Being . . .

can recognize that pain . . .

allowing that experience to speak out to you loud and clear . . .

telling you easily . . . comfortably . . .

what it is you need to do . . . to follow yourself . . .

*A*nd your unconscious mind . . .

*can cause you to **be aware** . . .*

*of that pain **in a new way** . . .*

speaking out to you now . . .

showing you what you've been unable to see . . .

handing you the gift . . . of coming back . . .

to yourself . . .

to take care of that body . . .

that heart . . . that mind . . .

and when it's time for an end . . .

that sadness can feel like a pain, doesn't it? . . .

*and you can **watch** that **experience** . . .*

responding to that communication . . . that signal . . .

... trusting the rains will come again ...

earth itself can become parched and cracked . . .

attempting to stay alive there in the sparseness of the desert . . .

full of what might be a painful dryness . . .

*splitting **open** the earth . . . waiting . . . **allow**ing . . .*

***trust**ing the rains will come again . . .*

and quench the thirst . . . of the earth . . .

allowing . . . a healing . . . can occur . . .

*and **a new beginning to begin** . . .*

*P*erhaps even a tiny rose bud . . . can feel the pain . . .

of that knowing it's **time** to die . . . to being a bud . . .

and time **to open** . . . and allow full blossoming to come . . .

and your **unconscious mind** . . .

can continue now **sort**ing through **your experience** . . .

setting aside those knowings . . .

that are your **know**ings . . .

about death, pressure and pain . . .

uncovering that flow . . . **discover**ing their **value** . . .

while your unconscious mind . . .

learns that feeling of **trust** . . . **in** your own experience . . .

as **life** moves from death to life . . . and back again . . .

      from pressure to comfort . . . and back again . . .

    from pain to pleasure . . . and back again . . .

*W*hen you're in pain . . .

    you know you're in pain, don't you? . . .

      there's no one else to ask . . .

there's no need to read it in a book . . .

      why you just know . . .

        that experience . . . is yours . . .

     and you can trust your experience . . .

and perhaps life ... .

as it expresses itself through the trees . . . the flowers . . .

the birds . . . as they fly in the air . . .

*can cause your **unconscious mind** now . . .*

*to **recognize the value** . . .*

*learning how to use that **pain** . . . those **endings** . . .*

*that **pressure** . . .*

*even the birds know how to **use** the pressure of the*

air . . .

to soar among the clouds . . .

even the fish in the sea . . .

use the pressure of the deep waters . . .

*to **help** them swim . . .*

*to **be free to** move and **explore** . . .*

*the deepest realms of the **rich depths** there below . . .*

and even the little clams . . . that make their way . . .

know how to use pressure to move . . .

allowing themselves to travel where they want to go . . .

and even your own body knows . . .

how to use the experience of pressure . . .

to help you walk . . .

to lift up a foot and allow the pressure to shift . . .

onto that other foot . . . and carry you forward . . .

Some *human beings have even* **learn**ed, *didn't*

you? . . .

how to make use of that pressure *of the*

wind . . .

designing the sail on a boat . . .

to catch that wind and move across the sea . . .

allowing the pressure of the wind on that sail . . .

to create a space on the other side . . .

a space that can catch that wind . . .

and cause that boat to move with ease . . .

. . . that funny little piece of material called a kite . . .

*A*nd others have learned . . .   -

how to take that funny little piece of material called a kite . . .

running with it fast and hard until it's caught by the wind . . .

creating a vacuum right above the kite . . .

*allowing the pressure to **lift** it up . . .*

to heights . . . ***never seen before*** . . .

*A*nd your unconscious mind . . .

can **draw on** the power . . .

of ***your un-noticed experience*** now . . .

*creating **new ways*** . . . ***to relate to life*** . . .

*to **be aware** you can flow with that pressure . . .*

you can allow that pain . . . to guide you back to yourself . . .

*as you **watch** . . .*

***explor**ing . . . becoming aware . . .*

that you are . . . alive . . .

*dancing in this flow of **beginnings and endings** . . .*

lightness and shadows . . .

like the very air you breathe . . .

right here . . . right now . . .

coming in and going out . . .

and your unconscious mind can . . .

allow this unfolding . . .

returning into your awareness now . . .

what you were taught not to know . . .

only as fast or as slow . . . as is just right for you . . .

can trust your experience . . . to guide you now . . .

as you go ahead . . .

tep out of those old beliefs . . .

you know you're ready to let go of . . .

and invite your unconscious mind . . .

can **ground** *you in that* **new trust** *. . .*

taking root **in your experience now** *. . .*

revealing to you **life's patterns** *. . .*

that **are yours to know** *. . .*

because after all . . . it is your life, isn't it? . . .

and you can live your life, can't you now? . . . your way . . .

because you can . . . be yourself . . .

and there's nobody else you can be . . . comfortably . . .

*W*hile *your unconscious mind can continue this work . . .*

in it's own way and it's own time . . .

dancing it's own dance . . . singing it's own song . . .

painting it's own picture . . .

as you continue to **uncover** *. . .*

your **experience outside those old beliefs** *. . .*

can be trusted now . . . to guide you on your way . . .

as you continue . . . **prepar**ing *for that next step of the journey . . .*

on toward that destination . . . unknown . . .

and begin **to recognize** *. . . what it's time for you to see . . .*

your abilities . . . to live **life** *. . .* **with a fresh perspective** *. . .*

*A*nd *as the end of a journey draws near . . .*

a traveler may tire . . .

of the hurry and the bustle . . . getting to that destination . . .

and it's nice to know . . .

the end of the journey will come . . . and you can **relax** *. . .*

and **enjoy** *the journey itself . . .*

each new beginning springing forth . . . out of what is done . . .

*J*ust as the seasons change -. . .

one following another . . .

the shadow of the next season always waiting in the

wings . . .

readying itself for it's time to emerge . . .

the steps of your journey . . . one at a time . . .

unfold . . . in the rhythm that is yours, isn't it? . . .

and just as this journey . . . can continue to

prepare itself now . . .

to come to that destination . . .

of the conscious mind awakening here . . .

perhaps to something it might have forgotten to

remember . . .

while the **unconscious mind** continues . . .

its own work now . . . allowing that trust . . .

your own experience . . .

will **create those new guildlines** that are yours . . .

in your own way . . .

and in a few moments now . . .

you can begin to **feel** the energies . . .

awakening and re-orienting that awareness . . .

toward this time and this place . . .

perhaps even feeling the energies returning . . .

*into the body **here** . . .*

*as if a new surge of life is coming into the body **now** . . .*

*as if **awaken**ing from a deeply **refresh**ing sleep . . .*

ready to begin the next stage of the journey . . .

as you go on your way . . .

taking with you what you'd like to keep . . .

*and **coming** gently and **easily back** . . .*

to this time and space . . .

wide awake . . .

right here** and right **now.

wake up!

Chapter 4

CONNECTIONS: In And Out – Alone And Together

As I walked toward Annie's room, I could feel a sense of separateness looming all around me. Everything and everyone close seemed to be moving away. All my feelings of connection were dissolving. The only sense of closeness still real was Annie.

I was buzzing with questions. Is everything really a part of a whole, or is it just a dream dangling in an impossible future? My connections always seemed to dis-connect, my closeness shifting into distance, my joy of being together changing into the desire for being alone. Are all these changes related? Am I really a part of any larger whole? The need for answers began to stalk my mind.

The pull to be with Annie was strong, and as I walked into her space, I could once again feel the deep relaxation begin. I couldn't doubt the truth of my connection with her, and that experience alone gave me hope. I felt myself surrendering to her unspoken invitation of rest. I knew she would guide me, as always, through the questions of my mind deep into the mysteries of my soul. I breathed deep as her words began to awaken yet again that special connection between our hearts.

*N*icholas, my friend,

Begin to find that comfortable position now . . .

yet once again . . .

just **allow**ing your attention to take in the sounds . . .

all around you now . . .

perhaps the position of your **body** as it **rest**s . . .

aware of the fact that what you're resting upon . . .

can support that body, can't it? . . .

*A*llowing the sensations . . .

to begin to **merge** and mingle with the sounds . . .

right along **with the feel of** these words . . .

as you continue to **let go** . . .

of any excess tension left from the day . . .

you can allow yourself to slide on down the sounds . . .

inside that **deep**ly receptive place . . .

that **comfort**able place deep **within** . . .

that you're continuing to **learn**, aren't you? . . .

is your place within . . .

that place where your **unconscious mind** can . . .

begin to move through those experiences . . .

that are **your experience of connections** . . .

*B*eginning now to **sort out** those knowings . . .

that are **your knowings** . . . and continue to **allow** now and

in the future. . .

those **beliefs** . . . rooted so strong and so long . . .

to loosen their hold . . . as your unconscious mind . . .

creates the **foundation** . . .

to allow these **new guidelines** . . . can take **shape** . . .

as the **facticities of importance** . . .

to you . . .

can begin to echo . . .

down through the corridors of time . . .

because for all time the human body . . .

has had its own way . . . of **reflect**ing that **connection** . . .

of the **outside with that inside** . . .

for where does a body's outside stop . . .

and where does a body's **inside** start? . . .

for is the **outside** inside . . . or is the inside out? . . .

the human body has its connections . . .

to the outside . . .

through that nose . . . that throat and mouth . . .

those tubes carrying that air and food . . . **connect** that body

to the outside . . .

*O*r do **those spaces** connect . . . the outside

to the **inside?** . . .

and regardless from where a person **looks** . . .

the **connections exist**, do they not?. . .

just like the human face . . . has many parts . . .

that stand out when a person's eye **searches** the mirror . . .

catching **a glimmer** of the eye or the nose . . .

the shape of the mouth . . . the set of the jaw . . .

each seemingly to be itself set apart from the other parts for

awhile . . .

and yet . . . the human face is a whole . . .

and **the whole** face is **more** . . .

than the sum of all the parts that are connected . . .

to allow that face . . . to be itself . . .

comfortably . . .

*J*ust as a person might remember . . .

how the organs of the body work . . .

to make certain each system functions well . . .

causing that breath to come and go . . .

the food to be received and digested . . . .

each organ . . . composed of single cells connected . . .

each working in it's own way . . .

to allow the whole to happen . . .

*and although a body can't **see the connections clearly** deep*

inside . . .

*why the body can **feel the presence** . . .*

of a whole system working . . .

and begin to trust your experience now . . .

the connections will occur . . . the connections can continue . . .

just as the egg that gives birth to the embryo . . .

*begins to grow . . . **connecting** itself **with a part** of itself . . .*

*that **splits** and becomes a self . . . that is a **separate** self . . .*

*and the two self cells do connect . . . and **together** . . .*

***allow the development** of the whole . . .*

*as the **connect**ions continue . . . **again** and again . . .*

***expand**ing . . . **extend**ing . . .*

echoing through the corridors of the body-mind . . .

*to allow . . . the whole . . . to **be at ease** . . . with knowing . . .*

the connections are there . . .

*each **allow**ing . . . **the whole** to be what **it is** . . .*

as a whole . . .

ven that little fish with the funny name . . .

the portuguese man of war . . .

*is **not** at **war at all** . . .*

just a single group of cells . . . attached to a hollow float . . .

each cell . . . with its different job to do . . .

and such a funny name to give a system that's

***peacefully** at **work** . . .*

*through **those connections** . . .*

*   **allowing** a **wholeness** to be . . . fully expressed . . .*

and of course . . .

in the waters of the sea in which the fish swim . . .

*lies the very **depth** . . . of the highest mountain peak . . .*

*for even the highest peak . . . **remains connected** . . .*

***to the** deepest depth of the earth . . .*

*the islands as they **peek** above the surface of the*

waters . . .

can trust their knowing . . . that deep beneath the surface of

*the **sea** . . .*

*they remain a part of **the** earth's **wholeness** of the planet . . .*

nd the depths **rest peacefully** . . .

  trusting their connection to that which is high

  above . . .

reaching toward the stars . . .

toward those skys where the birds can fly . . .

  everyone has seen a bird soaring in the sky . . .

    and some might think that bird feels unconnected . . .

      disconnected . . . and alone . . .

. . . alone . . . and yet connected together in a mysterious way.

*yet the birds that fly **together** in a flock . . .*

connect with each other in a mysterious way . . .

> *yet each free . . .*

*to fly in the only way you can fly on your own is **alone** . . .*

and yet . . . together . . . the birds create a formation . . .

*and fly through the skies together **connected** . . .*

*that form and shape remaining **a mystery to** the mind . . .*

> *and yet . . .*

*the birds can **feel** the connection . . .*

the pull . . . the direction . . . that guides them . . .

*where they're on their way to **reach that destination** now . . .*

*he skies can **relax with the journey** of the birds . . .*

> *leaving no tracks in its empty vastness there . . .*

the skies can feel the pull of the solar winds . . .

those clouds of dust . . . protons and neutrons . . .

produced by the solar storms . . .

moving outward from the sun . . .

affecting all those magnetic fields of the earth . . .

> *the moon . . . the planets . . .*

> *all together connected . . .*

> *to the stormy sensations of the sun . . .*

expressing itself . . .

the skies allow the sweeps of the solar wind to come . . .

the connections continuing . . .

as the movements of the sun . . .

effect the moon . . . the earth . . .

the very stars in the solar's system itself . . .

stars . . .

composed of the two most simple elements in that space . . .

hydrogen and helium coming together . . .

abundant in that vastness . . .

connecting . . .

taking shape . . .

and the other elements of this existence . . .

become alive in the interior *of the stars . . .*

and it's only under that deep pressure . . .

there on that inside . . .

the hydrogen and helium **come together** *. . . and* **create** *. . .*

deep in **the center** *of the star . . .*

the elements of the worlds all about . . .

When the pressure becomes the most . . . and it is time . . .

the star explodes . . . connecting itself with space . . .

expanding all around . . . as it seeds those elements . . .

throughout the vastness of the empty sky . . .

connecting like silver shiny threads darting out . . .

weaving a fabric of shimmering light . . .

as the connections . . . connect . . . and from these connections . . .

this very planet took shape . . .

this planet made from the stars . . . connected to the stars . . .

as are you . . . these elements . . .

perhaps seeded by a solar wind . . .

exploded by a star . . . expanding . . .

connecting themselves . . . with you . . .

or even the very smallest leaves . . .

express their pull toward the light . . .

lifting up their tiny tendrils toward the sun . . .

a natural connection to move toward the light . . .

*as the roots **honor** their **connections** . . .*

to the waters and move deep inside the earth . . .

*your **unconscious mind** can . . . begin to **recognize now** . . .*

*those **learnings that are yours** . . .*

*that can speak to you of **knowing** . . .*

***connections are real** . . .*

occurring even now . . .

*A**nd you can begin to trust your connection with life . . .*

*and **allow** that **connection to** . . .*

***disconnect** . . . **reconnect** . . . **connecting** . . .*

*allowing yourself to begin to **know** . . .*

*through **your own experience now** . . .*

you can trust your experience . . .

and continue to become aware . . . connectedness is

occurring . . .

*J*ust as the most beautiful flower is connected to its roots . . .

    the roots are connected to that flower . . .

        to **witness** that final expression of itself . . .

the fragrance . . . connected still with a threadlike whisper to

    that flower . . .

the fragrance free to connect with the winds . . .

        and move on its way . . .

to **allow the dance of connections to unfold** . . .

        in its own way . . .

now your **unconscious mind** can take these words . . .

these suggestions and directions . . .

to **sort through your experience** now . . .

and continue **becoming aware** . . . connections are

occurring . . .

*Y*ou can **use** these **knowings** . . . **that are yours** . . .

to **create** these new **understanding**s . . .

new guidelines . . . new ways to reach out . . .

and allow those connections in . . .

allow those connections to be . . .

and your **unconscious mind** is invited to do this work . . .

uprooting those **old beliefs** . . . loosening their hold . . .

creating the **space for a new connection** has **begun now** . . .

a connection that allows you to know . . .

*your connection **with life itself** . . .*

beginning with proof from that very breath . . .

*that **connects** you right now . . . from moment to moment . . .*

***with** that **gift of inspiration** . . .*

connections are ancient things . . .

*connections **go** way **back in time** . . .*

*and just as **there are** ancient connections . . .*

there can be ancient dreams . . . and just as there can be

*ancient dreams . . . there can be **ancient knowings** . . .*

***resting** there **deep** . . . **within** . . .*

*waiting for the right sound to **echo forward** through time . . .*

*and allow **a remembrance** to come now . . .*

of a very deep connection . . .

with the very experience of life itself . . .

... ancient knowings ... that are resting deep within ...

*J*ust as the very sounds that you hear . . .
are by themselves simply . . . floating in space . . .
yet connected together they become . . .
a full sound . . .

alive   with a feeling pulsating . . .

freeing you to feel the connection within . . .

around . . .

and beyond the sound . . .

becoming *aware* of the *connection* . . .

between *the* sound . . . *and the silence* . . .

allowing the feelings connected to those sounds can come . . .

ancient feelings of knowing . . .

something that the conscious mind can't quite find the words

to describe . . .

something the finger can only point to . . . but can't quite

touch . . .

***a deep connection . . . of meaning to you* . . .**

your connection . . . that echos through

your being . . .

*and an ancient connection is **a***

***connection that has a wisdom** . . .*

and that ancient knowing . . . can

reconnect . . .

with the now . . . and as the silence comes . . .

allow the sensations . . .

*to connect you **with that knowing** . . .*

you can be yourself comfortably . . . uncovering the rhythm

*that is your rhythm . . . **connecting with the movement and***

***flow of life** . . .*

that is your movement . . . and flow of life . . .

like the waters of the sea ebb and flow with the tides of the day . . .

*just **allow** . . . the **connection that is of importance to you** . . .*

*to continue **to take shape now** . . .*

finding its way to emerge . . . through the sounds . . .

up and out . . . of the silence . . .

onnections that you wish to know are your

connections . . .

*can **become available now to the***

***unconscious mind** . . .*

*to go ahead and **create** . . . **that understanding** . . .*

can be yours to know . . . yours to trust . . .

to feel the presence of that connection . . . with every breath

you take . . .

for in the knowing that you are connected . . .

you can relax, *can you not? . . .*

and allow the ebb and flow of life . . . to flow . . .

allowing . . .

*your **unconscious mind** the time and the space now . . .*

*to continue **loosen**ing the hold of **those old beliefs** . . .*

*and allow that **trust** . . . will continue taking shape . . .*

*using those knowings . . . that are **your knowings** . . .*

guiding you on your way now . . .

ecause your way is the only way for you . . .

to be yourself . . . comfortably . . .

and that connection . . . is your connection . . .

even as the sounds . . . the silence . . . the

sensations surround you now . . .

having connected you with a place within . . .

and even while within . . . connected with the without . . .

*you can **begin** to know that connection can remain . . .*

*as you begin this **process of reconnecting with***

*what's **outside** . . .*

which is connected to the inside . . .

because there is really no doubt, is there? . . .

what's inside is also outside . . .

and what's outside rests deep within . . .

in that place . . . that is your place now . . .

to connect . . . with yourself . . . and allow . . .

those ancient knowings continuing to arise . . .

n a few moments now . . .

*you can begin to **feel the energies** . . .*

***returning your awareness** . . .*

***into the body** . . .*

reconnecting . . .

your awareness . . .

with this time and place . . .

bringing with you, if you like . . .

a sense of knowing . . .

connectedness is a part of life . . .

*A*nd the connections ***flow*** *. . .*

just as the energies can flow . . .

into your body . . .

reconnecting that body with an energy . . .

that can carry you . . .

toward this time *. . .*

*and this place **now** . . .*

allowing you . . .

to reconnect with your awareness . . .

that can bring you into this time . . .

and this space . . .

***awaken**ing and enjoying your **right** to return*

*to right **here and now** . . .*

in your own way

and coming all the way alert now.

wake up!

THOUGHTS:

Lions In Wait

Chapter 5

THE FINGERPRINT DILEMMA - Uniqueness

As I entered her room, Annie's complete comfort with her differences struck me sharply. I was also fully aware of how much time she spent by herself, and the prospect of spending my life in that style didn't appeal. I was much more engaged with learning the art of moving slow in the fast lane.

My desire to be special to someone or unique in something, had begun to become a burden to me. I was vaguely aware that I was different from others, but somehow unwilling to receive this knowledge. Of course, being unique means there *is* no other like you - and to me, that meant being alone. I remembered Annie speaking of being both alone and together, and allowing the emergence of that courage to explore. I wasn't sure I was ready for such a revelation, but here I was once again.

She looked at me, waiting for some sign of what I wanted. I watched her, alert to my space of emptiness on the inside, and was suddenly aware of my fear to just be me. As my awareness arose, she beckoned me forward, as if she now knew why I had come. I could feel myself melting into the smooth rhythm of her voice as she spoke my name like no other could, calling forth that deep level of knowing I'd forgotten to remember once again.

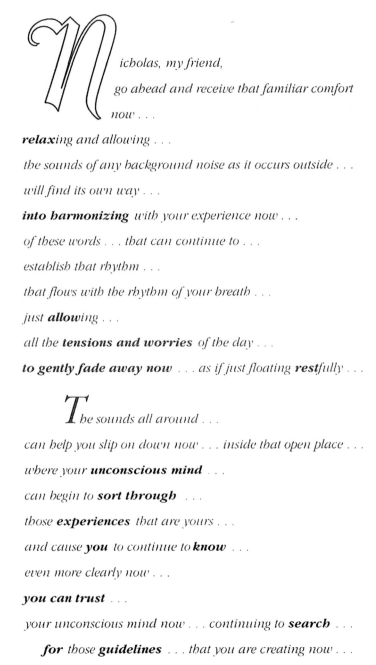

icholas, my friend,

go ahead and receive that familiar comfort

now . . .

relaxing *and allowing . . .*

the sounds of any background noise as it occurs outside . . .

will find its own way . . .

into harmonizing *with your experience now . . .*

of these words . . . that can continue to . . .

establish that rhythm . . .

that flows with the rhythm of your breath . . .

just **allowing** *. . .*

all the **tensions and worries** *of the day . . .*

to gently fade away now *. . . as if just floating* **restfully** *. . .*

he sounds all around . . .

can help you slip on down now . . . inside that open place . . .

where your **unconscious mind** *. . .*

can begin to **sort through** *. . .*

those **experiences** *that are yours . . .*

and cause **you** *to continue to* **know** *. . .*

even more clearly now . . .

you can trust *. . .*

your unconscious mind now . . . continuing to **search** *. . .*

for *those* **guidelines** *. . . that you are creating now . . .*

to allow *that* *uniqueness* . . .

that is the very expression of you . . .

to continue *to* *make its way forth* . . .

emerging in its own time and its own way . . .

only as fast or as slow now . . .

as you become ready to receive . . .

a deep *trust* . . . *that* *you* *too* . . .

are *a* *unique* *expression of life* . . .

like the morning glory . . .

trumpet shaped . . .

shouts out its glory to the morning sun . . .

free to *open* *and bloom throughout the day* . . .

and when the night comes . . .

the morning glory can close *comfortably* *now* . . .

having allowed its openness . . .

to be *expressed in its* *unique way* . . .

and the trumpet shape of that morning

salute to the sun . . .

seems to repeat itself . . .

with the moon flower of the night . . .

a trumpet shaped call to the stars . . .

yet the moon flower *moves beyond* *that*

seeming similarity . . . *that seeming*

repetition of shape and form to bloom in the night air . . .

fragrant with heart shaped leaves . . . *opening to the moon* . . .

*H*ave *you heard of that funny tree* . . .

in a far off distant land? . . .

the Baobob . . . blossoms opening into the light of the moon . . .

glimmering . . . a full tree . . .

enlightened with moon rich blossoms . . .

opening to the stars . . .

while the evening primrose . . .

so proper and precise throughout the

day . . . keeping closed as the daylight's

brightness parades by . . .

*relaxes **into** the soft night and opens* . . .

*in her **own** prim **style*** . . .

and there was a time . . .

when a certain person was known . . .

to have taken her knowledge of all the flowers of days and

nights . . . and consciously planted those flowers in her garden . . .

to create a flower bed clock . . .

the morning glory opening in the morn . . .

others opening with the noon day sun . . .

all the way down to the night blooming cirius . . .

and she could tell the time of day . . .

*by **honoring that uniqueness*** . . .

of each blossom as it comes in its own time . . .

in its own way . . .

*M*any times a **person** might feel . . .

that a blossom has to bloom in a certain way . . .

a blossom that opens to the sun . . .

or opens to the moon . . .

reaching . . .

spreading its petals to the sky . . .

and yet . . .

in a far distant land . . . there is a tree . . .

the Magnolia Wilson is its name . . .

that dares to blossom upside down . . .

the blossoms opening their petals toward the earth . . .

and to stand under a Magnolia Wilson tree . . .

is to be showered with flowers . . . as they bloom . . .

their fragrance releasing toward the earth . . .

and what seems like upside down to the earth . . .

is a right side up salute to the beauty of that uniqueness . . .

blossoming in its own way . . .

and in the night . . . the whipporwill sings its song . . .

the nightingale singing only when the sun has set . . .

keeping it's song a song of the night . . .

while many other birds sing throughout the day . . .

*and sometimes a person might **feel** like a mockingbird . . .*

imitating the calls and songs of others . . .

*not yet aware that even a mocking bird has a **song of***

*its **own** . . .*

that it can sing . . .

throughout the night . . .

... nature takes care... and allows each uniqueness...

*nd the **uniqueness** goes on . . .*

for although the mind wants to see all birds the same . . .

the same . . .

all birds that fly in the sky the same . . .

why that wonderful albatross . . .

having gotten the idea that it's a burden . . .

is a bird that was not built to fly at all . . .

*but rather **built to soar** . . .*

for the wings of that albatross are anatomically designed . . .

to lock in a position that frees that bird to soar . . .

like a glider sliding through the sky . . .

unable to fly with wings flapping . . .

*but **free to soar** . . .*

in a fluid flow with the wind . . .

*and nature takes care . . . and **allows** . . .*

*each **uniqueness . . . its place** . . .*

*why even the eyes that **shift** and change **perspective** in so many . . .*

are unique in that horse . . .

*that **change** of **focus** coming only as the angle of the head is shifted . . .*

and that's an unusual way to change a perspective, isn't it? . . .

What about that crocodile crying those tears . . .

and the crocodile does cry tears, you know . . .

expelling salt from the eyes . . .

or perhaps he is sad . . .

with his tongue so rooted to the bed of the mouth . . .

unable to move . . .

unlike the tongue of the snake . . .

so sensitive to sound it can vibrate . . .

and flicking that tongue frees the snake to listen . . .

picking up vibrations of sound . . .

without the ears you might have thought were needed . . .

and **hearing** **in** its **own** most **unique way** . . .

*S*ome people might think . . .

that all birds . . .

fly in the same way . . .

yet a hummingbird is the only bird . . .

that can fly backward into the unknown . . .

able to **find** its **way** around . . .

in a way that leaves other birds disoriented and confused . . .

and with blindness there . . .

that electric eel . . .

uses his electricity **naturally** . . .

to locate and stun its prey . . .

and ward off the dangers of the sea . . .

a stunning and shocking **experience** *. . .*

to see an eagle ray soar through the water . . .

propelling itself through the sea . . .

like the albatross glides through the air . . .

If a person cares to **look closely** *now . . .*

even those schools of humpback whales . . .

so seemingly the same to the

indiscriminate eye . . .

fashion the mark of

uniqueness on the

underside of each

whale's tail . . .

a unique pattern is

there *. . .*

and identifies each

whale as itself . . .

like the very print of your

thumb is **unique . . . in all**

the world *. . .*

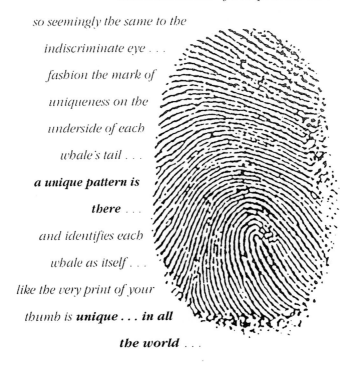

and just as all the parts of your face and your body . . .

are in and of themselves what they are . . .

*together they make **you . . . uniquely you** . . .*

*a part of a species that is . . . **the same and yet different** . . .*

*and of course your **unconscious mind** . . .*

***understands** . . .*

A s a pearl differs from all other gems . . .

you too differ . . . from all other beings . . .

for a pearl is also formed inside the shell . . .

soft . . . and absorbing . . .

as well as reflecting the light . . .

and sometimes people want to make a change . . .

and are so convinced there is a right way . . . to make a

change . . .

forgetting sometimes something seemingly miraculous can

occur . . .

why even dry ice . . . changes into gaseous vapor . . .

without doing what it would seemingly have to do first . . .

melting into a liquid flow . . .

and the uniqueness goes on . . .

just as the tongue deep within . . .

feels out the flavor of each taste . . .

keeping the bitter to the back . . .

the salty and pungent to the middle . . .

the sweetness resting there always . . . right at the tip of the

tongue . . .

knowing *the* **uniqueness** *of the taste* **is there** *. . .*

and all flavors have their place, don't they? . . .

and just how does . . . that sense of **know**ing *. . . know . . .*

you too are unique *. . . yet connected . . . right to life itself . . .*

for how does a seed **know** *as it moves in its journey . . .*

to carry itself to **parts unknown** *. . .*

to take root in a way of being . . .

not yet being the seed's to taste or see or feel? . . .

F or some seeds move by sticking to the pants of passers-by . . .

sticking to the coats of animals as they brush past the mother

plant . . .

other seeds hop and creep along

their way . . .

across vast expanses of land . . .

journeying toward a new home

where they can take root . . .

and **allow their uniqueness**

to come *. . .*

while other seeds tumble and tumble across the land . . .

some leap and ride the wind . . .

while others sink and float with the waves . . .

flying and riding on the winds and the tides . . .

while others very self-sufficient . . .

simply work very hard within . . .

until the time comes when they crack . . . and burst forth . . .

shooting out the seeds great distances . . .

where they can take root . . .

*and **allow** . . . **that uniquen**ess . . . to begin its journey . . .*

*toward **expression** . . .*

*I*t's curious to know . . .

when a person walks along the beach . . .

*sometimes **experienc**ing **a pull to** pick up the pebbles . . .*

othertimes a pull toward the colored rocks and shells . . .

*sometimes simply **delight**ing **in** the oozing, gushing feeling of
the sand . . .*

*each its **own unique beauty** creating the beach . . .*

the beach is all that is there . . .

the connections between the sands . . . the rocks . . . the pebbles . . .

the shells . . . the fish . . . the salt . . . the wind and the air . . .

*all together **connect**ed create the beach . . .*

*that place where you can walk **comfortably** . . .*

to connect with your own uniqueness now, can't you? . . .

for there is no other like you . . .

in all the world . . .

and there's nothing you can do about that . . .

    because that thumbprint is uniquely yours . . .

No matter how many members of the species are together . . .

    each connected in many ways . . .

that uniqueness remains with you now . . .

wherever you go . . .

*and your **unconscious mind** . . . can continue even now . . .*

*to **create** the **space** . . .*

*to **allow** those **old beliefs to loosen** . . .*

new experiences coming forth . . .

*as you continue to **recognize now** . . .*

you are you . . .

seemingly the same . . . yet, seemingly different . . .

*and **people are both**, are they not? . . .*

***alike . . . and different** . . .*

    and it's all right . . . to be yourself comfortably . . .

moving with the flow of moving yourself . . .

*to **recognize** now that uniqueness that is you . . .*

Because after all human beings have two eyes . . .
a nose . . .
two ears and a mouth . . . a forehead . . .
cheeks and a chin . . .

*but there's **no other** combination . . .*

exactly like you *rs . . .*

and that makes your face unique . . . doesn't it? . . .

and it's just that uniqueness . . .

all those things that you like and dislike . . .

that makes you you . . .

*and your **unconscious mind** now . . . will go ahead and
continue . . .*

*to **lay** the **foundations now** . . .*

*for you to **recognize** that uniqueness . . .*

*to **respect** . . . that one and only **expression of life** . . .*

that is you . . .

*to begin to **feel** . . . a **good** feeling . . .*

in knowing . . .

there's only one of you *. . .*

and existence, perhaps . . .

wants you to be yourself comfortably . . .

*and **allow** that uniqueness to emerge . . .*

blossoming *fully . . .*

> *allowing that fragrance . . . that is only yours . . .*
>
> *to dance with the wind . . .*

You are free to know . . .

> *you can move your own way now . . .*
>
> *enjoying the freedom . . .*
>
> *to continue uncovering . . .*
>
> *the uniqueness . . . of you . . .*

and it is nice to remember . . .

everything blooms in its own time . . .

*and your **unconscious mind** . . .*

*can take all the time it needs to **do this work** . . .*

sort*ing through **those experiences** that are yours now . . .*

*to **bring forth** those **guidelines** . . .*

*that can free you to **see** yourself now . . . **in a new light** . . .*

listen *to yourself . . . **with a new ear** . . .*

feel yourself . . . with a new sense of comfort . . .

because you are unique . . .

in all the world . . .

your unconscious mind has the ability . . .

to go ahead now . . .

*and **allow** that peaceful **healing** can arise . . . hasn't it?* . . .

because sometimes a wound can occur . . .

from a word or a look . . .

*that can cause a person to forget to **remember*** . . .

you are a unique expression . . . of life itself . . .

*an **open**ing . . . through which life breathes itself* . . .

> *hears itself* . . .

> *singing its song* . . .

> *sees itself* . . .

amidst . . . a field of colorful blossoms . . .

*F or how many times can a person **see** a field of flowers* . . .

*with no awareness at all . . . that **each** flower **is unique*** . . .

perhaps overwhelmed by the stunning beauty . . .

of a field filled with tulips blossoming . . . jonquils opening . . .

daisies dancing . . . overwhelmed by the vastness of all that is . . .

yet . . . if a person were to stroll through that field of flowers . . .

each flower's uniqueness would be revealed . . .

*each in itself . . . **essential*** . . .

for the whole** field of flowers **to be . . .

a field of flowers as it is . . .

every flower . . . having a role to play . . . a place essential . . .

for the creation of the whole to be . . .

without the part . . . there could be no whole . . .

without the whole . . . there could be no part . . .

and every blossom . . . though it blooms alone . . .

is a part of that whole . . . field of flowers . . . just being what

is . . . **allow***ing that*

overwhelming sight of **beauty** *to*

arise . . . and just as to an

untrained ear . . .

a symphony simply sounds like a

whole sound . . .

being sounded out . . .

to an ear trained to listen . . .

the absence of a single voice . . .

causes the whole to be less . . . than it was meant to be . . .

for even though ten flutes might be playing . . .

if the eleventh is silent . . .

the wholeness of the symphonic sound . . .

is not free to be heard . . .

and the loss is felt . . .

S*ometimes a person can feel lost . . .*

as if they are a piece of a puzzle that has no place . . .

wanting to **know** *their* **uniqueness** *and yet . . .*

only feeling different . . . left out of the whole . . .

yet everyone knows . . . that with a puzzle . . . every piece has

its place . . .

and sometimes it's a long time . . .

before just the right space . . .

that can welcome home that puzzle piece appears . . .

just the right shape . . . just the right form . . .

to allow that puzzle piece . . .

that thought it was just different and out of place . . .

with no where to fit . . . no way to find it's place there in the

puzzle . . .

*yet . . . now understood . . . a **needed** part **for the picture***

***to be whole** . . .*

*W*hen a bird flies on its wings . . .

it flies it's own way . . . doesn't it? . . .

because some birds have little wings . . .

and flap those little wings very very fast . . .

while other birds . . . with the same size wings . . .

move them a little bit slower . . .

while the hummingbird's wings go faster than any others . . .

and an eagle's wings . . . vast and broad . . .

expanding in the sky . . .

soar with very few movements . . . _

allowing the wind . . . to carry the eagle on its way . . .

and every bird that flies . . . flies alone, does it not? . . .

no matter how many fly together . . .

no matter what formation becomes free to arise . . .

they journey toward their destination in that certain shape . . .

*__each__ bird flying **alone** . . . **unique** . . . in its own space . . .*

creating its own path through the skies . . .

unique in the way it moves from here to there . . . to here . . .

*__yet connected with all__ the **others** who fly free . . .*

*and the **unconscious mind** . . .*

*can take these words . . . and **use these words now** . . .*

in the most appropriate and meaningful manner for you . . .

***allow**ing this **healing** . . .*

can deepen now . . .

inviting . . . a peacefulness can come . . .

*in **know**ing **you are unique** . . .*

in all the world . . .

every flower's scent . . .

being just its own flavor . . .

each dew drop . . . revealing its own reflection . . .

of the morning sun as it quivers on the tip of a

leaf . . .

each moment unique *. . .*

Y*ou too are a part . . .*

of all that is . . .

even as you breathe the very breath of life . . .

inspiring you just now . . .

to **feel the presence** *. . . of your unique self . . .*

in this garden of man . . .

each . . .

a flower blooming . . .

readying to share his fragrance . . . with the wind . . .

and the sky . . . and the stars . . .

readying to **reach beyond** *those* **limitations** *of mind . . .*

to **step past** *the* **beliefs** *. . .*

and **trust** *your* **new experience now** *. . .*

to **create** *for you the knowings . . . the* **understandings** *. . .*

the guidelines . . . the perspectives . . .

to guide you on your way . . .

is the only way . . . to **be yourself . . . comfortably** *. . .*

your unconscious mind can sort through those experiences . . .

gathering *those* **learnings . . .** *those* **resources** *. . .*

those **skills** *. . . that can heal the wounds of the past . . .*

and turn those energies now . . . toward **allowing** *. . .*

the **beauty of yourself** *. . .*

blossoming *. . .*

as you continue to know . . . your **experience is yours** *. . .*

to draw upon . . . to consult . . .

to **take with you now** *. . . wherever you go . . .*

*W*hen *existence can make every snowflake unique . . .*

perhaps you can trust all creations are unique . . .

creating themselves anew . . . fresh . . . with each breath . . .

and your **unconscious mind** *is invited now . . .*

to **continue** *this work . . .*

in the most appropriate and respectful manner . . .

for all the levels of your being you . . .

allowing *this* **healing** *will continue . . .*

allowing this trusting . . . your own **experience** *. . .*

can take root deeply now, can it not? . . .

even as you sleep at night . . .

unconscious mind always working . . .

*at a **deep** enough level . . .*

*to cause you to sleep **peace**fully . . . restfully . . . easily*

throughout the night . . .

awakening in the morning . . .

*as you're continuing to **awaken** here . . . feeling rested and*

refreshed . . .

and as your unconscious mind guides this awakening . . .

*to that **trust . . . in yourself** . . .*

you can allow this awakening continuing here now . . .

as you become aware that you can . . .

allow your unconscious mind to continue this work . . .

*even as you begin to feel the energies **re-orient**ing your*

awareness . . . right here . . .

*G*entfor *ently and easily returning **into the body** . . .*

*knowing as you have **awaken**ed many times . . .*

from dreams that you thought were real . . .

only to discover the dream was but a dream . . .

*you can allow awakening to continue occurring **now** . . .*

*as you become more and **more alert** . . .*

*these words calling your **awareness** to continue arising now . . .*

more and more toward this time and this place . . .

*feeling the **energy** . . .*

*coming back **in** to the body . . .*

*and every**body** has their own way . . .*

don't you? . . .

*of coming to a lovely **awaken**ed and **alive state** . . .*

*where you can **enjoy** what's going on in this moment . . .*

*in **this time** and in **this place** now . . .*

*and just let yourself now come all the way to right **here** . . .*

*wide **awake** and alert.*

wake up!

Chapter 6

BALANCE - Every Beauty Has Its Beast And Every Beast Has Its Beauty

It seemed I'd been struggling forever to find that place of balance - with my business, my relationships, my inner sense of self. And it seemed the more aware I became, the more unsteady everything seemed to be. With circumstances and people always shifting and changing, I felt incapable of holding that balance - with my temper, my desires, my centeredness itself. Whatever I had gained, I soon felt was lost. But I had begun to notice, just as Annie had said, the dance of duality unfolding, that pattern of movement *inside* the flow of change.

Still, this constant movement of life had me baffled. How to allow the movement and not get lost in the steady stream of shifting sands? How to find that place of balance and stay there? As I wavered between my doubt and trust that answers could be found, I noticed Annie enter the room. It was rare that I saw her move, although she spoke of her walks each day throughout the forest. Each step echoed the quiet grace of her beauty and there seemed no thing out of balance. Whether sitting or walking, Annie seemed to know how to allow the movement of life to be.

When she walked toward the window and her chair, everything in the room appeared to shift accomodating her presence. A harmony and balance I hadn't noticed those minutes before leaped out to greet her. She lowered her body into the chair like a leaf landing gently upon the ground, and allowed her eyes to rest on mine.

As I felt her gaze penetrate beyond my mind, the soothing sensations of rest began to arise. I could feel the tensions and worries melting into the harmony of the room, finding their place to rest quiet and unmoving, fading into pastel shadows of acceptance. As she began to speak my name, something deep on the inside returned to balance once again, and I breathed a deep sigh of relief.

Nicholas, my friend,

free your body to find that comfort now . . .

wherever you are . . .

let your attention shift just to your breathing for awhile . . .

*so you can **tune in**, can't you? . . . to your own rhythm now . . .*

*and **allow** your body to find its balance as you **rest** there . . .*

just allowing the sounds . . . and the sensations . . .

*to help yourself **shift inside** . . .*

*that much more **relax**ing state now . . .*

that place where those outside sounds of the world . . .

moving on their way . . .

can begin to blend with the sound of these words . . .

helping you to relax . . .

***accept**ing the **support** . . .*

*of what you're **rest**ing upon **now** . . . allowing . . .*

Balancing can come . . .

a balancing that allows . . .

that conscious mind . . . set aside for awhile now . . .

as if placed on an imaginary shelf . . .

creating space . . .

*for your **unconscious mind** . . . to take this time . . .*

*to **create** for you . . .*

the **space** . . .

to **allow** *the* **change***s* . . .

that you are ready to receive . . . can continue now . . .

readying themselves . . .

prepar*ing to come forth . . .*

*J*ust *as your conscious mind . . .*

may have had an idea about bringing you here and now . . .

your unconscious mind has its own reasons . . .

for bringing you to this time . . .

and this place . . .

and your unconscious mind can take this time . . .

to gather for you . . .

what you came here to receive . . .

from yourself . . .

in this time and space . . .

outside of space and time . . .

*Y*our **unconscious mind** *can even now* . . .

continue . . .

*to **sort through** that vast **realm*** . . .

*of your **experience*** . . .

*beginning to **gather** once again* . . .

*those **experiences** now* . . .

*that **can help** you continue **creating*** . . .

new ways . . .

***of** moving with the **balancing** of life* . . .

loosening those old limiting beliefs . . .

you through your own experience . . .

have come to know . . . you're ready . . .

*to **let go** of those **limiting beliefs*** . . .

*and **step into** that realm* . . .

*of **exploring** . . . **your experience*** . . .

allowing your unconscious mind the time . . . and the space . . .

*U*se *your experience now* . . .

*to **create new ways*** . . .

to allow that change . . .

***to** dance* . . .

*with the **flow*** . . .

of life . . .

from one . . .

extreme . . .

to the other . . . *extreme* . . .

to move through the shadows with an ease and trust . . .

in yourself . . .

that can allow that uniqueness . . .

to continue to be known by you . . .

trusting that connection . . . *with life* . . .

that comes with each and every breath . . .

is your connection . . .

moment . . .

to moment . . .

now . . .

*A*nd as your **unconscious mind** *moves now* . . .

to explore . . .

just how to **rearrange those old learnings** . . .

in new ways . . .

allowing what's been unequal . . .

can **come into balance** . . .

creating the space . . .

to allow the movement of your Being . . .

can move into balance now . . .

*L*ike *that time long ago . . .*

when you might have stood . . .

balancing on the edge of a curb . . .

standing there . . .

beginning to **experience how it feels to balance** *on the edge . . .*

pretending perhaps . . . as children do . . .

the curb is a tightrope strung high above the earth . . .

and you're walking on that thin line . . . strung tight across the sky . . .

and a person can feel the balancing begin . . .

as they walk . . .

perhaps on the track where a train runs . . .

balancing one foot and then the other . . .

holding out the arms to **allow the balance to come** *. . .*

first moving to the left . . .

then to the right . . .

and back again . . .

moving back and forth . . .

to find that moment of balance that comes and goes . . .

*F*or *balance is **a state of motion*** . . .

    you learned . . .

       simply walking . . . on that track . . .

the alertness needed to allow the body . . .

*can **re-establish** that **balance** . . .from moment to*

***moment** as you move* . . .

like walking on a tightrope . . .

knowing if the movement is too far toward one side . . .

a fall will be coming . . .

a movement too far to the other side . . .

a fall will be coming . . .

and the landing is seemingly always . . .

on another tightrope . . . where the balancing begins again . . .

just as the body . . . when it stands . . . continues to sway . . .

in its own way . . . back and forth . . . side to side . . .

continually recreating balance . . .

    allow**ing the **natural flow . . .

    ***from one side to the other** side* . . .

    to be the natural flow . . . as the

    balancing . . .

    allows the natural flow . . .

to balance . . .

to reach a state of constant motion . . .

where the balance returns . . .

as easy as breathing in . . . and breathing out . . .

alive . . . with life . . .

allowing the body to balance . . .

ven as the temperature of the body changes . . .

sweating lowering that temperature down . . .

allowing through evaporation that cooling effect . . .

*to **re-establish** the temperature to its **proper balance** . . .*

why even that ancient age-old response . . .

of the hairs on the arm . . .

lifting up as the pores tighten and expand . . .

*triggering that ancient knowing of how to **create** warmth . . .*

by causing that hair on the body to stand erect . . .

*an effort to restore the temperature to its **proper balance** . . .*

a movement that allows . . .

*the movement that is **natural to life** . . .*

to be what it is . . . allowing . . .

the plants, giving off that oxygen for people to breathe...

*J*ust *as the desire for food and thirst . . .*

allows *the **body to balance** . . . with just enough*

nourishment . . .

*to allow the **energy** to flow rightly . . .*

with just enough liquid . . .

*to allow the cells . . . **to be what** they **need to be** . . .*

why even the very muscles in the body . . .

have their own threshold . . . and balance in yet another way . . .

not responding at all to anything that is below that threshold . . .

and no matter . . . whether just at threshold or way beyond . . .

that muscle responds with its totality . . .

another balancing of all or none . . .

allowing . . . the balancing of each muscle . . .

to come to its rest . . .

preparing itself to act fully and completely and totally . . .

preparing itself to flow forth fully again . . .

and even the very cells of the body . . . **work to balance** *. . .*

those little charged particles . . . **positive and negative** *. . .*

rushing in and rushing out between the membranes . . .

allowing a balance to be restored . . .

after the job is done . . .

of allowing that impulse . . . to go on through . . .

*W**hy the very cells of the body* **understand balance** *. . .*

that **constant state of constant motion** *. . .*

allowing the changes to occur . . .

just as you breathe in and out . . .

the balance of exchange goes on . . .

between the plants . . . giving off that oxygen for people to breathe . . .

as they absorb the carbon dioxide the people exhale . . .

causing a balancing to come into being . . .

*J*ust *as the day and night . . .*

*in their **movement toward balance** . . .*

crawling through the long days of the summer . . .

do come to that time . . . in the autumn months . . .

where they balance . . .

equal lengths of day and night . . .

before they begin to stretch out again . . .

to reach that place . . .

*where they **come full circle** . . . **and balance** . . . yet again . . .*

allowing . . . the rhythm . . . of natural movement to be . . .

*B*ecause **when there's too much** . . .

like a cloud filled with too many electrons . . .

those electrons know it's time to leap to the earth . . .

and form that electric current seen as a flash of lightening . . .

releasing that stored up energy . . .

converting it into the heat and light . . . of the energy bolt . . .

***allow**ing a **balance** . . . in the cloud **to return** . . .*

like the explosion of the volcano . . .

when the pressure becomes too much . . .

reaches that place . . .

where the balance must be allowed to be restored . . .

And the releasing comes . . .

the explosion hot and red with its fury . . .

free to explode and change . . .

into that liquid flowing energy . . .

streaming with rivulet fingers of fire down the mountain side . . .

like a spring avalanche . . .

with the snows deep beneath beginning to melt . . .

the rivers of water beginning to form . . .

and what was once a solid mountain of snow . . .

begins to fall . . .

*as it changes form . . . **searching to restore a balance** . . .*

yet again . . .

it's curious to know, isn't it? . . . why even something. . . .

that takes one shape and then takes another . . .

has its same place of balance . . .

like an ice cube placed in a glass . . .

takes up as much space there . . .

whether it's liquid . . . or solid . . .

and a balance is maintained . . .

and how nice to know . . .

balance can continue . . .

*and your **unconscious mind knows** . . .*

*that **opposites** attract . . .*

*and when there's **too much of one** . . .*

*why the pull to move to **the other arises** . . .*

*and the **balancing begins** . . .*

allowing the movement that is natural to be . . .

L̲ike a juggler juggling . . .

*for once a juggler **understand**s the power . . .*

of his ability . . . to use a vision he'd perhaps not known was his own . . .

that peripheral vision allowing movement to be seen . . .

why then a person can look straight ahead . . .

and learn from the movement . . .

seeing its presence . . . allowing it to be . . .

***learn**ing **how** to hold the balls in the hand . . .*

allowing them to change . . . from one hand to another . . .

moving in a rhythm . . .

and once the rhythm of juggling is tasted . . .

*why a person can **remain in balance** with those balls . . .*

***with** that **constant flow of movement and motion** . . .*

like a juggler juggling...

you remaining balanced in the middle . . .

like the center of a storm . . .

and even on an island people learn . . .

when a tidal wave comes . . .

the safest place to be . . .

*is **the middle** . . .*

the center of the island . . .

***the balancing point** . . .*

that allows the natural motion to be what it is . . .

*while you **rest** . . . **in the center** . . .*

137

flowing with the gentle . . .

restoring of balance . . .

from moment . . . to moment . . . to moment . . .

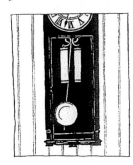
knowing a swing to the right holds

within it . . .

the seed . . .

of a swing to the left . . .

gathering its momentum like the

pendulum of the clock . . .

as it swings to the right . . . gathers the momentum to swing to

the left . . .

within each movement is the seed of its opposite . . .

and the balancing allows . . .

this equalization of what is . . .

E̲ven the birds that fly in the sky . . .

you know they use the pressure of the air, don't they? . . .

to help create their balance . . .

balancing with the pressure in order to fly straight . . .

to soar . . . to flit or flutter . . . or hover . . .

using their two wings to balance . . .

*as your **unconscious mind** can now . . .*

*use those abilities to learn . . . to **create** . . .*

to re-associate old knowings in new ways . . .

to allow **new understanding**s . . . can arise . . .

for **balancing is** . . .

a state of motion . . .

*J*ust as when the body wants to move . . .

a certain amount of tension must arise . . .

to **allow the movement** to occur . . .

yet . . . not too much tension is allowed . . .

or the movement is stilted . . . and loses its grace . . .

and the balancing goes on . . .

just as your very body has two divisions of that system

of nerves . . .

one to act under stress . . . to prepare for flight . . .

the other the deliverer of calm . . .

and they do work together . . . don't they? . . .

as they work in seeming opposition . . .

to allow movement to naturally occur . . .

it's curious to know . . .

most bodies in the universe that is known . . .

have an equal number of particles on the positive and negative

sides . . .

and when they come together . . .

they become uncharged . . . the body neutral now . . .

because of that balancing . . .

for when two opposites come together . . .

a particle and an anti-particle . . .

with equal force . . . meeting head on . . . so that both are

changed . . .

their energies convert . . . and shift . . . into other forms of

energy . . .

and that's quite a mystery, isn't it? . . .

*nd your **unconscious mind** can . . .*

*gather your **knowings about balancing***

now . . .

*and allow a new way . . . to come into **view** . . .*

*new words to be spoken . . . causing you to **hear** . . .*

*a new **grasp** on the power . . .*

*of **what it really means to balance in the middle** . . .*

free to move . . . with the movement . . . of the motion . . .

of the moment . . .

allowing . . .

*F*or *how easily a person can walk . . .*

yet in the winter time . . .

when the ground is covered with ice . . .

how the body does tense . . .

and how easy it is to fall on the ice . . . when the body tenses

too much . . .

*forgetting to **remember** its knowings . . .*

*about **relax**ing . . . letting go . . . and walking . . . with a*

gentle ease . . .

***allow**ing space for the **balancing to come** . . .*

why even the courts of old . . . kept a jester . . .

that court fool . . .

*to **bring balance** . . .*

and your unconscious mind knows . . .

***the feel of balancing** . . .*

and can use these words . . .

now and in the future . . .

in the most appropriate and powerful

manner for you . . .

continuing now to allow the letting go . . .

*of those **old beliefs** you're ready to **let go** of . . .*

*and allow your **unconscious mind** to . . .*

***use** your vast . . . pool of **experience** . . .*

to free you now . . .

to be yourself comfortably . . .

and allow the movement that is yours . . .

to guide you on your way . . .

to feel the feeling . . .

*of **moving with the way** . . . **things***

***are** . . .*

moving with your own energy . . .

allowing . . .

*O**f course your unconscious mind will continue this work . . .***

in its own manner, won't it? . . .

in its own style . . . in its own time . . .

*continuing to **sort** through that **experience that is yours** . . .*

***bring**ing those experiences **together** . . .*

***in creative and powerful new ways** . . .*

causing you to grasp with a new feeling . . .

to see with a new light . . .

to tune in and hear with a new ear . . .

what is yours now . . . to receive from yourself . . .

the knowings that are yours to allow . . .

to guide you on your way . . .

rusting . . . your own **experience** *. . . to guide you . . .*

to uncover what you want to know . . .

allowing the **balancing** *. . .*

simply aware of the process now . . .

that **every beauty** *. . .* **does have its beast** *. . .*

for the energies change . . .

flowing from one . . . side . . . of comfort . . .

to the opposite side . . . of discomfort . . .

and the wonder of knowing when the beast is present . . .

when the pain is raging forth . . .

when the agony is there demanding to be felt . . .

every beast *. . .* **has its beauty** *. . .*

for the **change will come** *. . .*

when discomfort has runs its course . . .

the comfort returning . . .

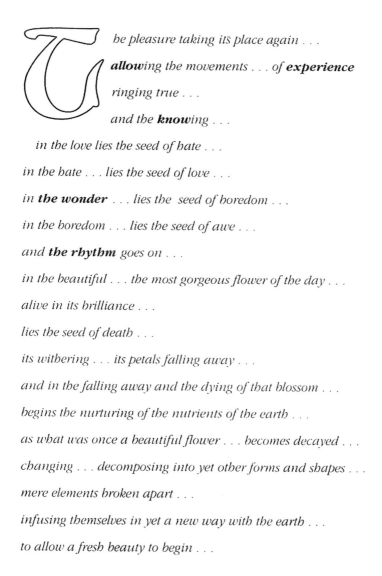

he pleasure taking its place again . . .

allowing the movements . . . of **experience**

ringing true . . .

and the **knowing** . . .

in the love lies the seed of hate . . .

in the hate . . . lies the seed of love . . .

in **the wonder** . . . lies the seed of boredom . . .

in the boredom . . . lies the seed of awe . . .

and **the rhythm** goes on . . .

in the beautiful . . . the most gorgeous flower of the day . . .

alive in its brilliance . . .

lies the seed of death . . .

its withering . . . its petals falling away . . .

and in the falling away and the dying of that blossom . . .

begins the nurturing of the nutrients of the earth . . .

as what was once a beautiful flower . . . becomes decayed . . .

changing . . . decomposing into yet other forms and shapes . . .

mere elements broken apart . . .

infusing themselves in yet a new way with the earth . . .

to allow a fresh beauty to begin . . .

Within every beginning . . . lies the seed of the end . . .

within every end lies the seed . . . of the beginning . . .

and the rhythm goes on like the breathing of life itself . . .

shifting . . . changing . . . yet the rhythm goes on . . .

whether a short breath . . . a long breath . . . a deep breath or

shallow . . . the balancing . . . comes in . . .

allowing the change . . . free to dance with the beauty . . .

to absorb its fragrant delights . . .

to move . . . with the majesty of the moment . . .

knowing within it lies its very demise . . .

like a bubble . . . fragile . . . yet full in its awakening . . .

and then bursting . . . there no more . . .

like a drop of dew in the morning . . .

there . . . and then evaporating into emptiness . . .

like a flash of lightening . . .

beautiful in its momentariness and then gone . . .

T he beauty of knowing the beast . . .

that resides within the beauty . . .

is allowing the beauty its fullness . . .

to be all that it can be . . .

savoring its presence . . .

for all that it is . . .

and when the beast arises . . .

allowing that beast . . . to be

what it is . . .

for it holds within the seed of beauty . . .

latent . . . invisible to the eye and yet . . . like a real seed itself . . .

you know holds the flower . . . not yet seen . . .

not yet free to share its fragrance . . . to flow with the wind . . .

yet the seed holds it safely there invisible to the eye . . .

*and **within every beast** . . . **there rests a beauty** . . .*

unseen . . .

within the anger rests the seed of compassion . . .

within the hate the seed of love . . .

within the jealousy the seed of freedom to be . . .

*only **able to flower** when the beast is given its time . . .*

***allowed** . . .*

and the cycle goes on . . .

*the rhythm . . . and **the balancing** . . .*

Like riding the see-saw up and down . . .

why a person can sit on one end or the other . . .

and move with the rhythm up and down . . .

***enjoy**ing the sweet swing into the elevation of **that height** . . .*

as the see-saw carries them up . . .

***the wonder of the** movement **down** . . .*

as they come and crash into the earth . . .

with that bump that makes you know you're down . . .

r a person can stand in the middle of the

plank . . .

allowing the ends to move in their natural

rhythm . . .

all the way up and all the way down . . . while that person

rests *. . .*

*balancing **in the middle** . . .*

allowing the movements . . .

free to be with those movements . . .

*to **allow** the adjustments to occur . . .*

*to flow with **the rhythm** of the see-saw swinging up and down . . .*

and the balancing is free to be felt . . .

*when a person **stands in the center** . . .*

allowing . . . the natural flow . . . to unfold . . .

*A*nd *your unconscious mind is invited now . . .*

to make maximum meaning of all these words . . .

in the most appropriate and meaningful way for you . . .

for within your beauty perhaps rests a beast . . .

seemingly raging to emerge . . .

perhaps within your beast rests a beauty . . .

awaiting its time to unfold . . .

and your unconscious mind can guide this process now . . .

of being yourself . . .

comfortably . . .

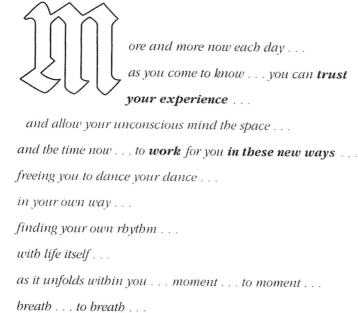

ore and more now each day . . .

*as you come to know . . . you can **trust***

***your experience** . . .*

and allow your unconscious mind the space . . .

*and the time now . . . to **work** for you **in these new ways** . . .*

freeing you to dance your dance . . .

in your own way . . .

finding your own rhythm . . .

with life itself . . .

as it unfolds within you . . . moment . . . to moment . . .

breath . . . to breath . . .

an inspiration to feel . . . a gift to receive . . .

your life to live . . . in your own way now . . .

*J*ust as you've allowed a balancing to occur . . .

that freed you to shift from that other state . . .

inside this deeply **relax**ed place within . . .

you may begin now to **become aware** of the energies

beginning to shift . . .

causing a movement to be . . . **gently** felt in that body . . .

just as you feel the energies shift in the morning . . .

as you prepare yourself to **awaken** . . .

from a deeply relaxing and refreshing sleep . . .

allowing the energies to rise . . . in the morning . . .

through the body . . .

knowing you can awaken refreshed . . .

alert and energized . . .

yet . . . in touch . . .

with something that was touched . . .

in a way that can allow you to know you can be yourself . . .

and be aware of that experience . . .

as beauty shifts into beast . . .

and beast transforms into beauty . . .

*and you can begin to just be **more aware now*** . . .

of the rebalancing as it is occurring . . .

***feel**ing the **energie**s continuing to shift*

bringing you** more and more gently and easily **back to this

time

and this place

*knowing you can **awaken** here*

refreshed . . .

***alert**, and relaxed.*

wake up!

BALANCE – Every Beauty Has Its Beast And Every Beast Has Its Beauty

THOUGHTS:

Chapter 7

A TREE OF TRUST - Rooted In Experience And Beyond Belief

Even then, as I stood paused in the emptiness of the doorway, I could feel the fullness of my experiences just across the threshold, and knew I was doubting them as valid and real.

This dance between doubt and trust bothered me deeply, for I knew the very truth I was seeking didn't have to be believed. I somehow knew I could experience what I was searching for. I needed to trust my knowing that it could be found, and found nestled right here in my experience of right now.

Annie gestured to enter the room, her simple movement somehow freeing my spirit to soar. How could I not trust these experiences that allowed me to taste my own beauty and grace and love? How could I not explore the wisdom being shared with that invitation to trust my experience and accept myself fully? As always, Annie somehow knew of the conflict within me. As she spoke my name, I could feel the seeds of trust I had asked for continuing to nestle down just a bit further into the receptive soil of my soul.

icholas, my friend,

just go ahead now . . .

and let your body find that comfortable position . . .

and know it doesn't really matter whether you move or remain still . . .

for your unconscious mind has brought you to these words . . .

for its own reasons . . .

and whatever thoughts your conscious mind might have . . .

it's free to follow those thoughts . . .

knowing your unconscious mind . . .

is going to do the work it came here to do . . .

acquiring for you . . . what you've come here to receive . . .

And your unconscious mind . . . can be aware . . .

that body can relax . . . in its own way and in its own time . . .

just allowing now . . . yourself . . .

to shift those gears from that day busy with movement . . .

into a gear that allows relaxation can come . . .

freeing your unconscious mind . . .

to take this time . . .

to create this space . . . for you to go ahead now . . .

*and **allow** . . .*

*the **opening of doors** you might **not** have even **known** were*

there . . .

freeing sounds and sensations . . .

*that can **guide** you now . . . with a **new, fresh direction** . . .*

*to be free **to float forth** . . .*

perhaps . . . on the background sounds . . . perhaps in a vision . . .

or a movement . . . embedded between the sounds . . .

***rest**ing deep . . . **within** the silence . . .*

*as you allow yourself . . . to **relax** . . .*

*C̶ontinuing to **explore** how it feels . . .*

*to allow your unconscious mind this time to **learn** . . .*

*for your unconscious mind has learned **many things**, won't*

it? . . .

and is free now . . .

to take those learnings . . . old and new . . .

*and begin to **build** . . . that **new foundation** . . .*

*solidly holding the **roots** beginning to come forth . . .*

*from **that seed of trust** . . .*

planted deep within your being . . .

a trust . . .

***in your un-noticed experience** . . .*

*a trust . . . **in yourself** . . .*

Because you may not **remember** that there
was a time . . .

before you even knew you could stand on
your own two feet . . . your unconscious mind learned
that learning . . .

and went on to **trust that learning** . . .

that experience **of** discovering . . .

how to **balance** there **support**ing yourself . . .

and **used that learning**, haven't you? . . .

to take you on and delight you with that experience of walking . . .

carrying you on to a time when you could move in a vast
variety of ways . . .

just like the time you might have been sure . . .

you'd never learn to make sense . . .

of all those funny scribbles and lines and circles on that paper
there . . .

that someone else said could have meaning . . .

and yet . . . despite any amount of frustration and difficulty . . .

you learned . . . how to distinguish a B from a D . . .

and went on to make those words . . .

those sentences . . .

and a whole new world opened to **explore** . . .

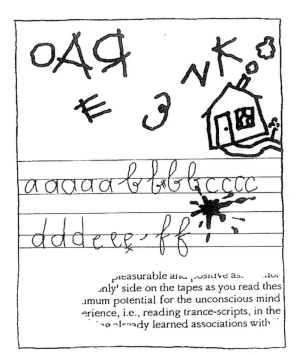

pleasurable and positive as ... to...
only' side on the tapes as you read thes
imum potential for the unconscious mind
erience, i.e., reading trance-scripts, in the
o already learned associations with

...to make sense of all those funny scribbles on that paper...

and as you read these words . . .

your **unconscious mind** *. . .*

regardless of the words being read . . .

can hear the words you need to hear . . .

to allow **this** *new tree of* **trust** *. . .*

to begin to take root . . . **in that experience** *. . .*

and just like your body . . .

uses that spinal column to support and keep you erect . . .

allow*ing those vertebrae to realign freely . . .*

that central core empty . . .

*but for **the** fluid that **flows** there . . .*

fluidly liquid . . .

helping to absorb the natural shock . . .

of movement . . .

*that tree of **trust** can begin . . . to take root . . .*

and allow itself to become a central core . . .

*as **solid yet flexible** as that spinal cord itself . . .*

filled with the fluid liquid flow of that trust . . .

in yourself . . .

*nd of course your **unconscious** mind*
brought you here . . . now . . .

*to continue **sort**ing **through** your **experience** . . .*

setting aside those experiences now . . .

*that can help you **explore** that **possibility** . . .*

*you can **trust** . . .*

***your own process** . . .*

your unfolding . . . your learnings . . .

*as you continue to **learn** . . .*

and allow that unconscious mind . . .

to use your experience now . . .

to **create new ways** . . .

that's right . . . **to relate to** *this experience* . . .

of experiencing your **life** . . .

in your way . . .

allowing those **old beliefs** *you're ready to let go of* . . .

continuing to **gently uproot** *themselves now* . . .

creating the space . . .

for those **new guidelines** . . . *to* **come** . . . **clear** . . .

firm . . .

in tune . . . *with all that you are* . . .

*I*t's *curious to realize* . . .

as existence unfolds itself day by day . . .

even the sun . . .

expresses itself in a new fashion each time it's time to rise . . .

dramatically allowing itself to set each night . . .

with new combinations and bursts of color . . .

and your unconscious mind can . . .

begin to **be aware** . . .

that seed of **trust can continue** . . .

to change into that seedling sprouting those roots . . .

reaching out . . .

toward just the right experience for you to trust and know . . .

you are also . . .

that part of life . . .

that continually moves . . .

    changing . . . dancing from one side to another . . .

A *nd your unconscious mind . . .*

    like the very soils of the earth . . .

      can continue creating the right soil now . . .

to allow that seed to take root . . .

and develop . . .

allowing *that* **trust** *. . .*

to come *to a blossoming . . . aren't you? . . .*

because a bud . . .

can open and flower . . .

and the seed that comes before . . .

may be like a bulb the gardener plants in the fall . . .

allowing itself to **rest** *deep in the earth . . .*

prepar*ing through the winter to bud in the spring . . .*

using the pressures of the winter . . .

needed **to develop** *that strength . . .*

to allow that bulb to open and come up through the ground . . .

*A*nd throughout the spring and summer . . .

those roots *deep in the earth . . .*

continue to prepare that bulb . . .

to produce a new flower again next year . . .

and the changes begin long before . . .

a person becomes aware . . .

that the blossoming is occurring . . .

*O*f course most people know . . .

that every seed has within it . . .

a blueprint of its future . . .

yet if the seed is dissected . . .

can you find the flower? . . .

can you find the fragrance? . . .

*so the gardener **allows** the seed its privacy . . .*

*and **trusts** . . .*

the blossoming will come . . .

attending to all he can do . . .

to provide the right soil . . .

*to **allow the journey** . . .*

*of that seed **to unfold** . . .*

   into blossom . . .

      into fragrance . . .

         into fruit . . .

nd of course often times . . .

a person might forget to remember . . .

how easily movement can occur . . .

because some movements in life . . .

come from a response . . .

to the light and the warmth of the day . . .

like the bear's knowing when it's time to hibernate . . .

becoming aware when the temperature changes to just the

right degree . . .

and that proportion of day to night is just perfect . . .

the bear trusts its knowing that it's time to sleep . . .

and **allows** *a deep* **rest** *to come . . .*

nd even the birds know to accept . . .

the basic limiting factors of their world . . .

and migrate when the time comes . . .

when the food becomes scarce . . .

and the weather too cold . . .

those birds **trust** *their* **inner knowing and change** *. . .*

where they live . . .

so they can **live more fully** *. . .*

*and there are **rhythms** of movement . . .*

that have nothing to do with the external world . . .

***of light and dark** . . .*

*of **warmth and cold** . . .*

because even a tiny bean seedling . . .

*lifting its leaves at daybreak **stretching** toward the sun . . .*

and lowering those leaves at night when it falls . . .

*the bean seedling **continues** this movement . . .*

even in constant darkness . . .

*following its intrinsic, **intuitive rhythm** of movement . . .*

and some plants . . .

***allow that mysterious process** . . .*

of photosynthesis . . .

changing that light

into energy . . .

comes to its peak in the midday sun . . .

and drops to a low at night . . .

yet even when there is no light . . .

*the plant uses its **learn**ings . . .*

*of **how to transform** and create that energy . . .*

and many seeds . . .

even when left in an unchanging place . . .

will germinate and grow faster in the spring and summer . . .

***regardless of what's** seemingly **going on** . . .*

*nd it's curious to **realize** . . .*

*these **intrinsic rhythms** flow . . .*

in their own rhythm . . .

***allow**ing a **process** to occur . . .*

***that is natural** . . . just as those little tadpoles in the water . . .*

hatch out of those eggs . . .

and breath through gills . . .

as they grow changing . . .

the tail absorbed . . . legs developing . . .

the shape and very color of the body . . .

beginning to resemble that adult frog . . .

changes in the skull, the skeleton and the intestines . . .

And it's interesting to know . . .

there is a destruction . . . isn't there? . . .

a rearrangement of all that was . . .

as something new comes into being . . .

*when that caterpillar **rest**s deep . . .*

in the womb of the coccoon . . .

***trust**ing . . . that **process** . . .*

why the caterpillar can only trust, can't he? . . . the process . . .

***to transform** . . .*

and carry it through to that not yet known freedom . . .

to fly the skies . . .

you know how to learn . . .

*you know how to **move** with those learnings . . .*

***into comfort**able positions . . .*

allowing those learnings have become a foundation now . . .

that can free you to flow . . .

***creatively exploring new ways** . . .*

***to be** at ease with yourself . . .*

f course anyone who's spent time learning . . .

all those creative things that can be devised in a kitchen . . .

knows all those years of flipping through the pages of the cookbook . . .

***collect**ing recipes . . .*

***and** exploring herbs and spices . . .*

*all **blend** together . . .*

creating the day . . .

*when a person can trust their **experience** there . . .*

and walk into any kitchen . . .

*and **create** a tasty, succulent delicious dish . . .*

and it's curious to know . . .

as many times as a person might go ahead . . .

*and **enjoy** the taste of bread . . .*

a seemingly **simple combination** *of ingredients . . .*

coming together *. . .*

*why that process can be **richly creative** . . .*

producing corn bread, rye bread, leavened and unleavened . . .

enriched, white, brown, oat . . .

chapati and tortilla . . .

differings shapes and sizes . . . all flowing freely . . .

*from a **trust** . . .*

*in **that experience** . . .*

when those basic ingredients . . .

come together in just the right way . . .

a unique kind of bread can happen . . .

*A*nd *your **unconscious mind** . . .*

is continuing to use these experiences now . . .

*to help you **relax** with change . . . can't you? . . .*

***trust**ing that **process** of movment as it unfolds . . .*

carrying you like the waters of the river . . .

from the right bank to the left . . .

***know**ing that water runs downhill . . . doesn't it? . . .*

and moves . . .

in a way that carries that water . . .

*to return to its **source** . . .*

And just as a person tense and tight . . .

in a fight with the water . . .

might think the river is out to swallow him alive . . .

*someone who knows how to **relax** . . .*

can float in that water . . .

allowing it to carry him on his way . . .

***trust**ing the ability of that water . . .*

. . . knowing that water runs downhill . . .

to support . . .

*to free that **deep relaxation** . . .*

to occur . . .

and sometimes a person forgets to trust . . .

becoming concerned . . .

that they are something . . .

not a part of all the rest that is . . .

seeing themselves perhaps like the unsightly orchid cactus . . .

a gangly, tendrilly, long and ugly plant . . .

to many an eye . . .

yet that plant allows itself to move . . .

through that process of being . . . that unsightly plant . . .

allowing . . .

the time to come . . .

the process to unfold . . .

when those beautiful blossoms burst forth . . .

staggering in their beauty . . .

round, brilliant, long trumpeted flowers . . .

with a deep throat . . .

all colors of the rainbow shouting with petals galore . . .

just as someone who learns . . .

how to dive inside the depths of the sea . . .

*comes to **trust** their **learnings in that environment** . . .*

*freeing them to **move** . . .*

with *an ease and comfort-and* **alertness** . . .

as they rely on their learnings about that world . . .

to help them survive and move easily . . .

free to **become aware** . . .

to **explore** *the beauties of* **the depths** . . .

as they unfold . . .

ometimes a person can spend a lot of energy and time . . .

gathering information and gathering skills . . .

and there once was a person . . .

who wanted to build a boat . . .

so badly did they wish to sail on their own . . .

that they took months and months and months . . .

that grew into years . . .

to gather all the information needed . . .

about the best kinds of wood . . .

the best kinds of nails . . .

the best shape and form . . .

took the time to learn the skills . . .

to go ahead and become a good carpenter . . .

and then bought those materials and took a year . . .

to build that boat . . .

and then sat . . .

on the dock . . .

and wondered if that boat would sail . . .

nd one day that man knew . . .
how it felt to sail out to sea . . .
trust*ing his own work . . .*
*his own experience of **learn**ing and doing and **creat**ing . . .*
*and that's a learning that might be of **value** . . . isn't it? . . .*
*to someone **watching** and listening . . .*
*creating their **own world** . . . their own movement . . .*
*of **allow**ing . . .*
*that **learning to unfold** . . .*

and your unconscious mind will continue now . . .

making maximum use of what has been heard here . . .

in a way that's appropriate for you . . .

and that mind can . . .

create a way now . . .

to give you what you came here to receive . . .

*while even allowing that tree of **trust** . . .*

will continue taking root . . .

*in **your experience** . . . unnoticed up to now . . .*

allowing your unconscious mind . . .

is working for you . . . ***in new ways*** *. . .*

trusting . . . yourself . . . learning . . .

upon learnings . . . upon learnings . . .

it's ok to ***be*** *. . .* ***yourself*** *. . . comfortably . . .*

   flowing into that calm . . .

   that ability to ***relax*** *. . .*

      with change . . .

      trusting . . .

that because you know ***change*** *. . .*

is everywhere . . .

you can relax with that change . . .

F reeing your unconscious mind . . .

to continue to know now . . .

it's all right to ***explore*** *these new ways . . .*

of relating to change . . .

moving into exploring your ability . . .

to dance with ***your own process*** *. . .*

relaxing . . .

allowing the energies to flow . . .

like the pendulum of the clock . . .

from one extreme . . .

      to the other extreme . . .

utilizing the momentum as it builds . . .

to carry itself on to the other side . . .

freeing that circle . . . to complete. . . .

in your way . . .

B*ecause your unconscious mind can . . .*

*sort out those **experiences** that free you to*

remember . . .

*with **every end** . . .*

***is a new beginning** . . .*

and within each beginning rests the seed of the end . . .

and even the leaves that fall from the tree . . .

***continue** on their way **to nourish** . . .*

the roots . . . of that from which it came . . .

and it's curious to realize . . .

even those birds have learned . . . haven't they? . . .

how to trust the pressure of the air . . .

to help them fly . . .

to free themselves to soar . . .

and sometimes . . .

why the pain of that shell around the seed cracking open . . .

is freeing something that's been held within . . .

to find its way . . .

toward a new place . . .

to continue on its own . . .

journey toward fulfillment . . .

And your unconscious mind can continue . . .

to allow these learnings . . . these knowings . . .

that are your knowings now . . .

to continue coming together . . .

creat*ing for you . . . **new ways to relax** with change . . .*

*to dance **with** those **opposites** . . .*

to step right on through the shadows . . .

*with a lightness and a **trust** . . .*

in yourself . . .

*because **that process** . . .*

is unfolding even now . . .

*each breath **inspiring** the next*

exhalation to come . . .

*allowing the **letting in** . . .*

*and the **letting go** . . .*

to complete . . .

freeing that process . . .

like the freshness of a spring bursting forth . . .

can spring anew with each breath . . .

as that tree of trust . . .

continues to take root deeply . . .

in your experience now . . .

trusting those experiences to help guide you on your way . . .

freeing yourself . . .

to move in rhythm now . . .

with what you've come to know . . .

about life . . . living itself through you . . .

nd as those energies loosen . . .

their hold . . .

on those beliefs . . .

allowing *these* **new guidelines** *. . .*

created by your unconscious mind . . .

rooted in *your* **knowing** *. . .*

your dis-counted experience*s . . .*

your learnings . . .

that energy is free now to flow naturally . . .

allowing that uniqueness . . .

continuing to be expressed . . .

for even though the sound of the flute is unique . . .

to itself . . .

a pure miracle to hear . . .

a symphony needs all of its parts to be played . . .

to allow the fullness to come . . .

*A*nd yes . . .

*your **unconscious mind** can . . .*

take anything that's been heard here . . .

appropriate and respectful for you . . .

right on with you now . . .

and continue . . .

*exploring, **developing**, **creating** new ways . . .*

to relate to this experience of experiencing life . . .

***ways** that free you **to** tune in and **feel** . . .*

***the rhythm of life** with every breath . . .*

as it breathes you anew . . .

freeing that vision to come clear . . .

that is your vision to follow . . .

***allow**ing the sound of your own silence . . .*

to have the time and space . . .

to speak to you . . .

*of **your own knowings** . . .*

and that **trust** . . .

is yours to allow . . .

to invite . . . *to join the dance* . . .

of **being yourself** *comfortably* . . .

because after all . . .

there is no one else you can be . . .

yourself . . . *comfortably* . . .

and you can **relax** . . .

into that uniqueness . . .

trusting . . . *perhaps you too* . . .

are a part of the whole . . .

*F*or *every part that is a part from the whole* . . .

might think that it is a part apart from the whole . . .

but the whole needs every part . . .

to be a whole . . .

and perhaps the part . . .

holds the whole within . . .

to be known . . .

*A*nd *your unconscious mind is invited now . . .*

*to go ahead and **continue this work** . . .*

in its own way . . . in its own time . . .

perhaps even as you sleep at night . . .

always working at a deep enough level to free you to sleep . . .

peacefully, restfully throughout the night . . .

*awakening in the morning as you're going to **awaken** . . .*

here very soon . . .

***refreshed** . . .*

wide awake . . .

alert . . .

knowing you really can take these learnings with you now . . .

*and trust your unconscious mind can **continue** creating . . .*

***exploring** . . . developing new ways . . .*

to guide you on your way . . .

allowing that tree of trust . . .

*to **move beyond belief** . . .*

*and root itself in **experience** that **is yours** . . .*

***to know** . . . to guide you on your way . . .*

*A*nd *in a few moments now . . .*

you'll begin to be more aware . . .

of the process of **shift***ing toward* **now** *. . .*

as an energy begins to arise . . .

that will carry you

toward *this time and this place . . .*

knowing when you come all the way to this time . . .

and this place . . .

like **awakening** *from a deeply refreshing sleep . . .*

you can bring anything you'd like with you . . .

all the way to right here and now . . .

perhaps even when you fully return . . .

to this time and space . . .

wanting to take the time to notice the sky above . . .

   allowing the process of that stillness in motion to unfold . . .

      as you watch that vast expanse before the eyes . . .

*and as you hear these words . . . a little **more** clearly now . . .*

*perhaps becoming a little more aware of the **energy** . . .*

*returning your awareness **into** that **body** . . .*

feeling your awareness coming in through your toes . . .

the top of your head . . .

maybe even through your fingers . . .

the soles of your feet . . .

*letting **energy** come more and more **now** . . .*

*bring **aware**ness and **alert**ness right into the body . . .*

*as you **come** all the way to **here** and now . . .*

wide awake and alert.

wake up!

Chapter 8

USEFULNESS - Is This A Gift?

I could easily experience Annie, her room, and our times together as a gift. But so much of the rest of my life seemed beyond any useful purpose. It often appeared like the meanderings of a lost soul climbing to heights and plummeting into valleys, journeying toward that ever elusive horizon, always as far away as ever.

People often spoke of life as a gift, but I didn't really experience it that way on the inside. It was such an effort to take those moments of darkness and make them useful. It often seemed such a simplistic approach to the complex phenomena of life. Yet, I could see those who lived life in this way were more relaxed and at ease with whatever experience arose.

As I stood at the door, I was suddenly aware of Annie. Her body was silhouetted in inky black against the winter's sky, her outline shimmering golden in its play with the setting sun. At that moment, I somehow knew life was simply what it was. Whether a gift or a punishment, it was happening and it was happening to me. These moments dissolved my mind into awe, leaving me quiet and still, my questions melted into knowing, my trust emerging, silent and strong.

In that spacious and mysterious moment beyond time, Annie motioned me forward. As I settled inside myself, the soft strength of her words, once again, carried me toward home, my own knowings simply waiting there like a gift to be received.

*N*icholas, my friend,

just allow that comfort once again . . .

and if you'd like . . .

you can **allow** your attention to begin to move . . .

from the **awareness** of the sounds around you now . . .

allowing your attention **to shift** with those sounds . . .

into those sensations of comfort . . .

allowing all the sounds to help you slide on down now . . .

into the feeling of that surface just beneath you . . .

feeling its **support** . . .

and as those sounds and sensations . . .

and thoughts in your mind . . .

become like . . .

ripples in a pond . . .

flowing on out and out . . .

from the place where the pebble plops . . .

through the surface of

the water . . .

allowing the ripples of

sounds and sensations to

flow on out now . . .

freeing the energies to **calm** . . .

like the surface of that pond becoming still . . .

when the ripples have gone their way . . .

*and as that **stillness** begins . . .*

***begin**ning to perhaps feel the silence . . .*

cradling the sounds all around . . .

like the depths of the pond . . .

cradle that surface . . .

*you can begin to allow your **learn**ings now . . .*

***to** help you **relax** and **accept** that support . . .*

of what you're resting on . . .

*perhaps even **feel**ing . . . a feeling . . .*

*of **appreciation for** that support . . .*

*holding **you** . . .*

cradling you now as you rest . . .

allowing . . .

*your **unconscious mind** the time . . .*

and the space now . . .

*to **take** that **next step** . . . of going on now . . .*

*and **exploring** that **experience** . . .*

that is your experience . . .

*that can begin to give you a sense **of knowing** . . .*

***new ways to relate** . . .*

*to experiencing **your experience** . . .*

*ften times when a person begins to **notice** . . .*

*various **things** in life unnoticed before . . .*

*why a person can begin to **be aware** . . .*

of how many places life . . . expresses itself . . .

in a manner that appears . . .

to have a use . . . a role to play . . .

a function to fulfill . . .

like that hermit crab moving there in the waters by the sea . . .

uses that conch shell in which it lives for a long time . . .

to protect . . .

that soft . . . uncovered abdomen . . .

and when the crab outgrows that shell . . .

why . . . that shell . . . is no longer useful to that crab, is it? . . .

and the crab is free to go on its way . . .

*the shell also **free** to become a home to another . . .*

*A*nd of course . . .

in the waters of the sea . . .

those funny animals called otters . . .

are known for their **playfulness** . . .

running and tumbling and rolling in the waters of the sea . . .

and some might think that playing has no use . . .

yet . . .

any mother otter **knows** *the* **value** . . .

of teaching her children . . .

how to move and flow . . . with the waves **of** *the water . . .*

an ability easily learned while **playing** . . .

*A*nd of course . . . *the waters of the brook . . .*

distinctive in its babbling that goes on and on . . .

can only be heard . . .

because of the rocks resting there . . .

and for another . . . those rocks might only be rocks . . .

yet for the brook . . . the rocks allows its song to be sung . . .

...the rocks can become stepping stones...

*A*nd for a person with an eye that can see . . .

why the rocks in the brook become **step**ping stones . . .

used to help a person cross . . .

from one place to another . . .

and the stones upon which a person steps . . .

can be different stones for different people . . .

for a **step**ping stone . . .

that's used to help a person cross . . .

is chosen by the walker . . .

as they progress along the distance . . .

      toward where they want to go . . .

*A*nd yes . . . the sounds all around . . .

sometimes can crash loud . . . and seem disturbing . . .

and yet . . . sometimes the sounds . . .

alert the silence to awaken . . .

to **a new depth of being present** . . .

like the owl at night . . .

with its silent flight . . .

uses the sounds . . .

that leap out of the silence . . . to **guide** it to its prey . . .

to free that hunting to be done . . .

with precision . . .

and of course that owl knows how to use the dark . . .

for the night provides protection for hunting . . .

for eating . . .

for many wild life animals to survive they must move in the
night . . .

it's safe inside the night for the coyote and the owl . . .

like the darkness of the sea . . .

frees the crab and octopus . . .

to come up into the darkness of the night . . .

Sometimes a person has many feelings . . .

about being given something they have to **learn**

how to use . . .

and it's curious **to watch** . . .

even the kangaroo with its big tail . . .

learning how to keep that tail on the ground . . .

yet using its presence for pushing off . . .

because without that lift . . .

why the jumping cannot occur . . . can it? . . .

and even that earthworm . . .

had to **learn how to use** those muscles it was given . . .

putting **pressure** on the fluid in its body . . .

to make itself move . . .

and it uses that pressure . . .

like the birds of the sky have to **learn** . . .

how **to value** that **pressure** of the air . . .

using it to fly and soar free . . .

how to use those feathers in the tail . . .

to tilt and spread and close . . .

and guide them on their way . . .

*W*hy even the very **body** . . .

    knows how to make use of pressure . . .

for that very circulation flowing through the body right now . . .

  occurs through pressure that keeps those liquids moving . . .

    that very **breathing deeply** . . .

    is a function of that pressure . . .

    and gravity working together now . . .

    allowing that hot air to rise . . .

    that cold air to sink . . .

    and the learnings are there . . .

*A*nd it's curious to **be aware** . . .

a person doesn't ask to hear the light . . .

for you know your ears aren't made to **see the light** . . .

a person doesn't ask to see music, do you? . . .

because a person knows your eyes can't hear . . .

and it's curious to become aware now . . .

the function of the mind . . .

is to create those questions . . . those doubts . . .

that skepticism and suspicion of what's to come . . .

and the function of the heart . . .

*to give and **receive** . . . and to love . . .*

and I wonder if a person can learn . . .

to only ask . . . of each part . . .

*that which is its **ability** to do . . .*

for when a person asks the eyes to hear . . .

and the ears to see . . .

*why a person is asking something that's beyond the **capacity** . . .*

and limitations of what is there . . .

and sometimes a person can feel . . .

the capacities of that adrenalin beginning to flow . . .

adrenalin caused to flow by stress . . .

causing a person to be faster and more alert . . .

like the predators in the wild . . .

that adrenalin helpful to that wolf in the wilderness . . .

to catch his food and avoid being eaten . . .

*why that adrenalin is a **powerful, useful thing to have** . . .*

And sometimes a person can look to the future . . .

and because of that looking into the unknown . . .

why a person might miss the experience of being

in the present . . .

and what is a present but a gift . . .

*and how does a person **receive** a **gift**? . . .*

why everyone knows . . .

to receive a gift . . .

a person allows the present . . .

to be received . . .

and a person then . . .

can appreciate the present . . .

*and a person can **open the present** . . .*

*and a person can **explore the present** . . .*

*and **enjoy** and **delight** in the present . . .*

*and **realize** the present is not the past . . .*

***the present is a gift** . . .*

and when a person receives a present . . .

why they can have many feelings, can't they? . . .

while remembering . . .

the present is a gift . . .

***to be appreciated** . . .*

the present is a gift . . .

*to be **received** . . .*

*and whether **that gift** . . .*

is a gift you wanted . . .

or a gift . . . you didn't desire at all . . .

a gift is a gift . . .

and a person can learn to receive the present . . .

***in a whole new way** . . .*

and the very usefulness of an empty bowl...

Sometimes a person can learn . . .

how it feels to just receive . . .

and allow what's present to come . . .

like an empty bowl . . .

allows its ***emptiness*** to hold anything . . .

and it remains unaffected . . .

and the very ***useful***ness of an empty bowl . . .

does come, doesn't it? . . .

from its ***ability to allow*** that ***emptiness*** to hold anything . . .

and remain unaffected . . .

because if a bowl remains full . . .

*why it's not **available**, is it? . . .*

***to fill up with** anything fresh and **new** . . .*

*S*ometimes . . . *filling the night skies . . .*

the very stars in their twinkling and glimmering . . .

might look forward . . .

to the coming of the sun once again . . .

freeing them . . .

*to **become more light** . . .*

to melt into the light of the daytime sky . . .

***free**ing the **power** of the sun **to shine** full . . .*

and sometimes a star might want to hold onto the night . . .

even as the dawn is beginning to break . . .

*and yet the stars have **learn**ed . . .*

*to allow themselves to **let go** . . .*

and slide on inside the brightness of the day . . .

and the brightness of a vision . . .

that vision of what can be . . .

can become so bright sometimes it can hurt the eyes . . .

and a person learns to close the eyes, don't they? . . .

and allow the brightness of the sun to be . . .

yet protecting those eyes so they can see . . .

nd your unconscious mind can continue . . .

to sort through those experiences . . .

that are your experiences . . .

reach *in and touch . . .* **a deep remembrance within** *. . .*

that **every part is a part of the whole** *. . .*

and you can **move** *in your part now . . .*

because life and its activity on earth . . .

depends on that transformation of energy . . .

from less useful forms . . .

to more useful forms of energy *. . .*

that atomic energy and radiant energy . . .

electrical energy and chemical energy . . .

heat energy and mechanical energy . . .

all working to **transform** *themselves . . .*

into other forms of **energy** *. . .*

each **more useful than the one left behind** *. . .*

opening itself to explore . . .

opening *itself to move . . .*

with *an* **appreciation** *. . .*

of **allow**ing *. . .*

that **transformation** *to come . . .*

hose green plants taking that radiant energy

from the sun . . .

and allowing it to change . . .

into the form of a chemical energy . . .

and human beings and other animals move . . .

by changing chemical energy within that body . . .

into mechanical energy that moves those legs . . .

and the very electricity of life is created . . .

by changing that mechanical energy of water running . . .

into that electrical energy . . .

and changing heat energy into the form of electricity . . .

and the cycle goes on . . .

each part having its role to play . . .

*each part **learning** . . .*

***how to** move with what is . . . its experience in life . . .*

*is yours now . . . to **draw upon** . . .*

because you've made it this far, haven't you? . . .

*and you've left **many experiences** behind . . .*

like many suits of clothes out grown . . .

*moved on into new ways of **being yourself** . . .*

comfortably now . . .

moved on into tasting the delight . . .

*of **receiv**ing a present . . .*

> as a **new way of receiving these moments** . . .
>
> *as they unfold before you* . . .

Because it's all right now . . .

to **explore** *how it feels to be like the seasons* . . .

fully living the moments of **each**

experience . . .

springing forth brand new and fresh **with aliveness** . . .

budding forth . . .

slowing on down into the sultry, smoothness of the summer

heat . . .

that slides and melts its way into the colors of fall . . .

as they begin to burst boldly through that greenness of the

summer . . .

and as the cold, hardness of winter comes . . .

the autumn **relaxes** . . . **into** *the womb of the cold* . . .

crust of the earth . . . **allowing** . . .

the **gifts** *of winter* **to come** . . . **in their own way** . . .

silent and deep beneath the surface of the earth . . .

the gifts of the cold darkness of winter go on . . .

preparing . . . *nourishing the very seeds* . . .

that will burst forth and blossom in the spring . . .

*A*nd just as every sound and silence . . .

every sensation and feeling and taste has its place . . .

when it occurs . . .

fulfilling a role it is there to play . . .

you can **relax** *. . . and begin to* **trust your experience** *. . .*

that what was once useful that you've now left behind . . .

will be useful to another . . .

freeing you to **let go** *. . .* **of what's done** *. . .*

and **receive the present** *as it unfolds . . .*

opening *itself before your very eyes . . .*

eyes you can allow to **see** *what's there now . . .*

ears you can free to **hear** *what's being said . . .*

a body you can free to **feel** *itself . . .*

alive with **life** *. . .*

*E*ach moment **unfolds anew** . . .

the sounds and sensations flowing in a pattern . . .

allowing . . . **each part** . . .

*to play its part **as a part of the whole*** . . .

while the whole is whole . . .

*for **each moment** . . . is present to itself* . . .

*and **free to be received** as a gift* . . .

and when a person learns, can't they? . . .

what the very birds of the sky already know . . .

why then a person can . . .

use that pressure all around . . .

to go ahead now . . .

*and **transform*** . . .

allow that pressure to lift you up . . .

and free you to soar in the skies . . .

*because **what's no longer useful*** . . .

can simply be set aside . . .

and you can rest assured . . .

*as you move on into **accept**ing and receiving* . . .

the feel of the present that's given you . . .

*to **experience*** . . .

because you know how to receive a gift . . .

*you can **use that knowing now*** . . .

and **explore your ability** . . .

to receive your experience as it unfolds moment to moment . . .

a gift . . .

each moment . . . with a role to play . . .

in the nourishment **of** your **awakening** . . .

to your **trust** . . . in **yourself** . . .

*Y*es . . . sometimes even what is seemingly

beyond a person . . .

seemingly out of reach . . .

can be grasped . . .

and free a person to **expand** . . .

allowing themselves . . . to **extend** . . .

beyond a place . . . they thought . . .

was a **limitation** . . .

and your unconscious mind now . . .

can go ahead . . .

continuing to soothe the very being

of your Being . . .

sorting through those dis-counted

experiences . . .

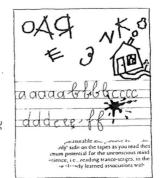

drawing upon those **knowings** . . .

those **learnings** . . .

because you've learned how to receive a gift, haven't you? . . .

and you can continue . . .

to **explore your abilities** . . . *to* **relate** . . .

to your experience *of life* . . .

as **a gift** . . .

for you to use . . .

to discover and **explore** . . .

what's *there for* **you** *to* **know** . . .

f course your unconscious mind will do this work . . .

in your way . . .

because there's no other way to be . . .

but your way . . .

is the way . . . *for you* . . .

to be yourself comfortably . . .

moving toward that **trust** . . .

in **yourself** . . .

and when a person can learn, didn't you? . . .

to flow with the moments of life . . .

like the fish of the sea flow with the waves . . .

and the turbulence of the waters themselves . . .

*why a person can begin to **trust** . . .*

*their **ability** . . . **to** receive . . .*

*in the way that makes you **feel good** . . .*

And your unconscious mind will continue this work . . .

in its own way and its own fashion . . .

*just as you've learned to make **use** of these restful times . . .*

freeing those deep levels of your mind . . .

to have the time and the space . . .

*to explore **your ability** . . .*

to take those steps . . .

*that can cause you . . . **to recognize** your gift . . .*

*an expression of **life unfolding** . . .*

like the very stars at night . . .

shine their light . . .

creating a gentle darkness . . .

while the sun sleeps . . . resting . . .

preparing for the time to shine fully alive again . . .

uring these times, you can know . . .

*your **unconscious mind** moves with*

*you . . . you can **take** these **learnings** . . .*

*these **knowings** . . . these **rememberings** right on with you . . .*

your unconscious mind continuing to take these steps . . .

to do this work . . . just as there is your way . . .

to begin to wind your way . . .

back toward this time and this place . . .

***becom**ing more **aware** of these words now . . .*

a useful guide to that place deep inside . . .

*where **transformation can occur** . . . hasn't it? . . .*

allowing these words as you begin to make your way now . . .

toward here and now . . .

***becom**ing **aware** of how the energy shifts and flows in the body . . .*

as you feel the energies of awakening present . . .

coming more and more into the body . . .

***know**ing **you can awaken** here as you awaken in the mornings . . .*

*refreshed, rested, **relaxed**, energized . . .*

***aware of each moment** now . . . as you return . . .*

to the experience that is your experience to savor . . .

feeling the sensations . . .

the enlivening of all the muscles in the body now . . .

as you come to that place of re-orienting . . .

coming to right here and now . . .

*where you can **feel** . . .*

*the **desire to stretch** those muscles arising . . .*

and feel them claiming their function . . .

*of helping you to **move** . . . once again . . .*

freeing you to stretch on into this time and this place . . .

gently and easily . . .

*coming all the way **to here and now** . . .*

wide awake and alert.

wake up!

Chapter 9

CONSCIOUSNESS - A Catalyst for Life

As I stood at Annie's window, I was overcome with fatigue. I was constantly striving to be aware, putting out enormous efforts to re-create my balance and increasingly worried that I would never be good enough or alert enough to reach my goals. It all seemed incredibly hopeless.

Annie kept reminding me to relax, but how could I when I was so far from where I wanted to be? I watched her pouring a cup of tea. Her grace and presence startled me once again. Could it be that relaxation was the key? Could it be all I needed to do was allow what was to be? Was it true that all I was striving for could not be attained, but only relaxed into and received? Was consciousness like the sea in which the fish swim, constantly present and around all the time? Relax into awareness and balance instead of striving to create it? The possiblity stunned my mind into silence.

With this confusion stirring, Annie handed me the tea cup, filled right to the brim. She smiled as the steaming liquid threatened to slide over the side and into the saucer. I knew she wanted me to simply shift my attention to right now, the same space as always that held the answers to my questions. I grinned and felt the relaxation flow again. Would I never stop getting caught in the meanderings of my mind?

With the tea warming my inside, I stretched out, waiting for the sweet sound of her voice to begin. As I waited, I could feel my awareness beginning to arise, wrapping its gentle fingers around all the sounds and sensations floating by, caressing and receiving even my thoughts and feelings. What had been waiting but a moment before, was suddenly transformed into living and I breathed a deep sigh of contentment as she began to speak my name.

*N*icholas, my friend,

you can invite your body . . . once again

now . . .

to find that   comfortable position . . .

any position you feel will allow you . . .

to just begin now . . . to **remember** . . .

how it feels to **relax** . . .

into the sounds all around you . . .

the background sounds . . .

the sound of these words . . .

*S*liding on inside those sensations now . . . as they arise . . .

allowing **that support** . . .

of what you're resting upon . . .

the **move**ment **within** the body as you breathe . . .

finding its way . . .

toward **your own rhythm** now . . .

just allowing yourself . . . to remember . . .

how it feels to **relax** . . .

to **let go** of each exhalation . . .

allowing a new **inspiration** to come . . .

relaxing into the very air that surrounds your **body** . . .

the very atmosphere in which you **live** . . . touching . . .

caressing the skin even now . . .

Y*et a person can remain un**aware**, can't they? . . .*

*of life's air **all around** . . .*

until a moment comes . . .

*when **consciousness** . . .*

of that slight pressure against the skin . . .

can move into the mind's eye . . .

allowing . . .

what you came here to gather . . .

to continue being prepared . . .

even through the noise of the mind . . .

your very Being can use this time now . . .

*to **continue exploring that awareness** . . .*

*and its **awakening** to your being . . . as you are . . .*

right now . . .

the key now . . .

that awareness . . . that consciousness . . .

*your unconscious mind beginning to **explore now** . . .*

*this **possibility** . . . that **awareness is yours** . . .*

*to use . . . to **step in**to . . .*

anytime you remember now . . .

for life itself all around lives . . . in the atmosphere . . .

*that **nearly transparent** envelope . . .*

of gases and particles surrounding the earth . . .

...the atmosphere shielding the earth...

the **atmosphere** *playing a crucial role* . . .

in the very existence of life . . .

for **that** *atmosphere* **exists all around** . . .

enveloping with its transparency . . .

yet transporting . . .

water from the oceans to the land itself . . .

transmitting radiation from the sun . . .

so essential to those green plants being **free** . . .

to turn that light . . . *into* **energy** . . .

the atmosphere shielding the earth . . .

from those lethal ultra-violet rays and meteor showers . . .

acting as a blanket . . . covering the earth . . .

maintaining her temperature . . .

cooling the torrid heat of the tropics . . .

warming the barren coldness of the polar regions . . .

nd that atmosphere moves . . . and carries sound . . .

*electromagnetic waves **allowing** communication to occur . . .*

that atmosphere . . . surrounding . . .

*an **essential key** . . .*

***to** the **unlocking** of **life** . . . itself . . .*

*and **somewhere** in that atmosphere **rests** . . . the sky . . .*

and can the sky be somewhere when it's everywhere? . . .

can the sky be somewhere . . .

specific . . .

*when the sky is always **here**? . . .*

why even behind the clouds that cling . . .

their grey darkness like a covering . . .

the sky remains vast . . . in its presence . . .

patiently waiting . . .

*to be **free** . . . **to come forth** again . . .*

Sometimes . . . *a person can become so accustomed . . .*

to the pull of that gravity from the earth . . .

so heavy and pervasive and unseen . . .

so habituated to that pull downward . . .

a person can forget to even **notice** *. . .*

that gravity's pull . . .

and a person might forget to **remember** *. . .*

there are ways to break loose from that pull . . .

because man has **learned** *now . . .*

how to fly, didn't he? . . .

to move in a plane across the skies . . .

and even in a rocket soaring . . .

into **new realms never explored before** *. . .*

experienc*ing* **light***ness . . .*

weightless . . . floating there . . . **free** *for the first time . . .*

from the pull . . . of that earth . . .

and that **awareness** *. . . like the light . . .*

can be free **to come in** *like the sky . . .*

as it appears behind the clouds . . .

the light . . . coming in . . .

causes the darkness to disappear . . .

*I*t's curious to become aware . . .

a person can't work with the dark . . .

why a person can't do anything with the dark . . .

a person has to work with the light . . .

and **allow** that **light to come in** . . .

and **free** the darkness to disappear . . .

why even the very **nourishments**

locked up in that refrigerator . . .

come into the light easily when you **open that door** . . .

and the light clicks on, didn't it? . . .

and you can **see clearly all that is there** . . .

because the darkness disappears, won't it? . . .

when the door opens and the light is brought in . . .

freeing a person to **see** clearly . . .

all the **nourishments** that were there all along . . .

*A*nd it's curious to **realize** . . .

that human eyes take a while . . .

to **adapt** completely . . . **to seeing in the dark** . . .

but once those eyes are adapted . . .

why the human eye naturally becomes . . .

a 100,000 times more sensitive to the **light** . . .

shining in the dark . . .

than they are in the bright sunlight of the day . . .

why even a tiny glow from a cigarette . . .

can be seen for hundreds of yards . . .

on a very dark night . . .

allowing a new way to be seen . . .

to move through that darkness . . .

seeing your way clear . . .

as those night eyes learn . . .

of their ability to see in the dark . . .

nd some people don't know . . .

there are substances in the world . . .

that give off light when they absorb energy . . .

substances that are phosphorescent and shine in the dark . . .

and those substances . . . allow their light to disappear . . .

when the energy source is removed . . .

but there are plants and animals that create their own light . . .

luminescent . . .

fireflies glowing as they fly . . .

glow worms shining as they move . . .

jelly fish lighting themselves up with delight . . .

why there's even a mushroom that glows . . .

and that lantern fish . . . living deep in the darkest part of the

sea . . .

where there is

no light . . .

at all . . .

why that

lantern fish

generates *its*

*own **self-illumination** . . .*

even there . . .

in the deepest, darkness of the sea . . .

> *allowing the water . . . to flow . . .*

*P*erhaps *you've never been aware . . .*

that the waters of the earth . . .

go on flowing with no guide . . .

no maps . . . no discipline . . .

why the waters of the river simply flow . . .

never going uphill . . .

always flowing downhill . . .

*always **reach**ing **toward** the ocean . . . their very **source** . . .*

and yet . . .

when water comes to a boil . . .

it begins to evaporate . . .

*and **moves upward** . . .*

*a **transformation** of **that energy** . . . flowing . . .*

In olden days . . . people tried to change . . .

the basest metals into gold . . .

the alchemy of transformation became its name . . .

yet the time is here, isn't it? . . .

*when that ability to **change** one element into another **has***

***occurred** . . .*

it's now been done . . .

the transformation of one element . . .

changing it right on into another . . .

fast paced accelerators . . . shooting those atomic particles . . .

right to the heart of the matter . . .

bombarding those atoms . . .

where an electric force . . .

acts on a charged body . . . in a certain way . . .

and magic seems to unfold . . .

and the chemists of not too long ago . . . ridiculed the idea . . .

yet now it can be done . . .

transformation can occur *. . .*

allowing what was once one thing . . . to become yet another . . .

nd that **awareness** *that* **is yours** *. . .*
can continue to **make itself more known**
now *. . .*

like that beluga whale . . . a small arctic mammel born black . . .

and as it grows . . . it lightens . . .

until it becomes pure white . . .

in its maturity . . .

and that **consciousness can** *. . . continue . . .*

to lighten . . .

and make itself known to you . . .

like the light of the lantern fish . . .

illuminating *the* **depths** *of the sea . . .*

like a piece of stone to a sculptor . . .

surrounds a hidden work of art waiting to be free . . .

and no matter what shape . . .

the sculptor **allows** *to come . . .*

the **center** *of that stone remains* **pure** *. . .*

remains untouched . . .

that awareness like the center . . . -

> *of a cyclone is always calm . . .*

*the center **untouched** by the raging forces of the winds . . .*

furious in their movement . . .

*A*nd *the center moves with the storm . . .*

as it arises . . . the center is there . . .

as it unfolds in its fury and movement . . . the center is there . . .

calm . . . untouched . . .

and as the storm dies . . .

*the **center remains** . . .*

to receive the winds . . . as they dissolve . . .

into the waiting arms . . . of the atmosphere . . .

*   **always there** . . .

    *as your **awareness awaits** your*

    arrival . . .

    like a calm, center of a storm . . .

    ***always there** before the storm . . .*

    during the storm . . .

    after the cyclone dispells itself . . . into

    the very sky . . . the center remains . . .

like the ocean . . . salty in the center . . . salty on the shores . . .

for wherever the ocean is . . .

as it surrounds, envelopes and engulfs . . .

the life that swims in the sea . . .

the taste of the sea is salty everywhere . . .

and do you suppose the fish . . . that

*live in the **sea** . . .*

are thirsty? . . .

or are they aware . . .

*of **that** very **environment** which*

*is their **home** . . .*

***supporting** and **nourishing** them*

through every moment of their life there? . . .

* S ometimes . . .*

a person might become like a tree . . .

a tree cut off from its roots . . .

and it's quite possible that a tree . . .

cut off from its roots . . .

might consider fragrance . . .

a mere fantasy . . . a tree cut off from its roots . . .

might consider flowers . . .

an illusion to be dispelled . . .

a tree cut off from its roots . . .

might feel no meaning in its existence there . . .

yet . . . a tree cut off from its roots . . .

is no longer connected with life itself . . .

and as that tree might watch another . . .

whose roots are deeply embraced by the earth . . .

filling itself . . .

with the very stuff of which life is made . . .

why that tree might watch another . . .

blossoming its flowers . . .

and might even smell the fragrance . . .

but without its roots . . .

that tree will never have its own flowers opening . . .

yet life, hungry to live . . .

finds its way . . .

even when the roots are cut . . .

to a new place . . .

where the roots can take root again . . .

and even the grass knows . . .

how to find its way through the hardness of the concrete

street . . .

to continue its reach for the skies . . .

*nd your **unconscious mind** can . . .*

begin to cause you . . .

*to **be aware** of that **awareness now** . . .*

like a mirror reflecting what is there . . .

*that awareness **arising** like a key . . .*

*to unlock that energy **that is your energy** . . .*

your potential energy that can be released . . .

like any object that's been bent or stretched or compressed . . .

*when **allowed** to **return** . . .*

to its natural form . . .

why . . . the energy's potential is released . . .

and your awareness . . .

is waiting there now . . .

like a host . . .

ready to receive the guests *that come and go . . .*

and the best host . . .

is the host who treats his guests graciously . . .

respectfully . . .

alert to their needs almost before they are . . .

and that awareness . . .

can be host to all that comes and goes . . .

*Y*es . . . *you know that experience of knowing*
don't you? . . .
that still . . . silent voice deep within . . .
that intuitive knowing that speaks to you . . .
from a place that rings true . . .
feels familiar . . . yet . . .
is transparent to the eye . . .
intangible to the touch . . .
silent to the ear . . .
yet you can hear the echo . . .

*F*or *what is an echo but a sound heard again . . .*
near its source . . .
as it **returns** *after being reflected . . .*
from some obstructing surface . . .
and that **awareness** *echoes*
now . . . throughout your being . . .
calling you . . .
to come home . . . to yourself . . .

to **relax** *. . .* **into** *the arms of that* **awareness** *. . .*
like **a gracious host** *. . . accepting all that is . . .*
without judgement *. . .* **without comparison** *. . .*

Because a person can spend a lot of time

flipping a coin . . .

even knowing that fifty percent of the time . . .

that coin will come up heads . . .

and fifty percent of the time . . .

that coin will come up tails . . .

and often times a person forgets to **remember** . . .

that a coin has three sides . . .

because there is also the rim . . .

balanced there between the two . . .

connecting the two sides . . . yet . . .

unaffected by which is heads and which is tails . . .

unconcerned . . . with how it falls . . .

because the rim between the two . . .

is balanced . . .

connected with both sides . . .

yet free . . . to remain itself . . .

to **remain free** . . .

of that game . . .

of heads and tails . . .

yet always **present** . . .

for the play . . .

nd I don't know exactly . . .

how your **unconscious mind** *. . .*

is going to take these words . . .

and continue **explor**ing *the* **presence of** *that* **awareness** *. . .*

like the very atmosphere **all around** *. . .*

allowing that awareness . . . to continue its process . . .

of **return**ing *you . . .* **to your natural self** *. . .*

like the very water and winds of the earth . . .

wear away . . .

the surface of the earth's soil . . .

a continuous process *of erosion . . .*

by natural agents . . . like the wind and the sea . . .

that awareness can continue . . .

To bring into the light . . .

what is naturally yours . . .

to become aware . . .

that you are . . . a part . . . that is a part of the whole . . .

and your unconscious mind can continue . . .

developing *that* **ability** *. . .*

to come to your senses *. . . and* **be aware** *. . .*

of yourself *. . .*

the seeing . . . the hearing . . .

the feeling . . . the tasting . . . the smelling . . .

because that of which you can be aware . . .

cannot be you . . . can it? . . .

for you are the one . . . being aware . . .

and perhaps that awareness . . .

is like the sky itself . . .

like the very center of the storm . . .

like the very air we breathe . . .

all around . . .

and you can continue to **remember** *now, can't you? . . .*

you can be aware . . .

    and **learn** *. . . to be yourself comfortably now . . .*

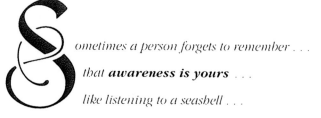

ometimes a person forgets to remember . . .

    that **awareness is yours** *. . .*

    like listening to a seashell . . .

      a person can be amazed to think the sound there . . .

is the sound of the ocean . . .

contained there in that shell held up to the ear . . .

and how can a shell . . . have the ocean's sound? . . .

and a person forgets to remember . . .

the sound being heard . . .

is the echo of your blood . . . pulsating in the ear . . .

like that awareness . . .

calling you now . . .

is within . . .

and without . . .

surrounding you . . .

like a blanket of warm coolness inviting you . . .

*to **step in** . . .*

*and allow **that awareness** . . .*

*to **unlock** the door . . .*

to a whole new way . . .

of relating . . .

*to **your experience** . . .*

of being yourself . . .

comfortably now . . .

.. dolphins have learned to dive deep...and surface...and dive...

*P*erhaps you can **discover** that **awareness** . . .

all around . . . like the very levels of the sea . . .

that the dolphins have learned to dive deep . . .

and surface and **dive deep** and surface . . .

playful and free to move . . .

in all the many levels of the sea . . .

the very environment and atmosphere of their home . . .

*A*nd that **awareness is yours** . . .

all around . . . and you can play . . . and

delight in this **explora**tion . . .

of your **freedom to be aware** . . .

more and more each day . . .

letting go . . .

relaxing in**side that remembrance** . . .

to come to the moment . . .

and **step into** that place . . . that is **your awareness now** . . .

relaxing . . . coming home . . .

to the very place . . . where you live . . . within . . .

*A*nd your unconscious mind is invited now . . .

to use all these words . . .

in the most appropriate and powerful manner for you . . .

can become free to remember . . .

you can be aware now . . .

of yourself feeling . . . seeing . . . hearing . . .

aware of the very miracle of life unfolding with each breath . . .

a gift to enjoy . . .

to allow . . .

yourself now . . . to **connect** with your very roots . . .

*A*nd free the knowing . . .

that it's your time to **know** . . .

to continue that journey . . . into **the light** . . .

and in a few moments now . . .

you will begin to feel an energy . . . calling your awareness

now . . .

to **come** into the body . . .

where it's been resting . . . inside and **outside** . . .

perhaps being aware of how it really feels **now** . . .

to return to this time and this place . . .

being here **in this environment** . . .

right here and now . . .

aware of how it feels to follow the thread of these words . . .

guiding you here to this time and this place . . .

aware of **feel**ing your **body now** . . .

*aware of **hear**ing the outside **sounds** . . .*

aware of preparing to see what is all around . . .

*perhaps just aware of **be**ing **alert** and present . . .*

*as you **awaken** now . . .*

in this time and place . . .

inviting the energies . . .

*to come all the way fully **inside the body now** . . .*

causing you to become now . . .

*wide awake and **alert**.*

wake up!

Lions In Wait

Chapter 10

NO-SELF — Is There Anybody Really Home?

Sometimes when my creativity was flowing, I had the strangest sense that it had nothing to do with me. I could almost see clearly that it was simply happening, each inspiration arising out of nowhere. Those times were incredibly fulfilling, and far beyond description and words.

I stood waiting, my question for Annie formed and precise. Is there really anybody here to learn anything or do anything?

It seemed I was finally tired of engaging in my fights to be right, to be the best, the most handsome and bright. There had to be another way to understand this sense of myself as separate, a way that could free me to let go and relax. My mind froze at the thought of not existing as me. And at the same time, I remembered the feelings of freedom and joy when I moved beyond myself out of love and by choice.

Annie moved into the room slowly. Sensing the moment's delicacy, she walked softly to the window and turned to face me fully. She gazed at me with incredible softness, her eyes empty save for the fullness of a presence I could not describe with words. I could feel this presence knocking on a door of my heart, a door that had been hidden even from me. As the door opened, I froze and melted simultaneously, and then let go . . . allowing her gentle words to guide me, once again, home to my own experience, even deeper on the inside than I had imagined possible.

*N*icholas, my friend,

you know how to allow your **attention** now . . .

to move from the sounds of the outside world . . .

shifting that awareness to your **body** . . .

resting here . . .

knowing that you can . . . if you like . . .

accept the **support** of what you're resting upon . . .

allowing that support . . .

to cradle your **body** now . . .

as you take **this time** once again . . .

to allow your unconscious mind the time . . .

and the space now . . .

to gather for you . . .

what you came here to **receive** . . .

*F*or while you've been **rest**ing here . . .

listening to those words and ideas . . .

why your **unconscious mind** . . .

has been **listen**ing as well . . . and **learn**ing . . .

that you can gather **for yourself** . . .

what you came here to receive . . .

*A*lthough *you may have had many conscious*

thoughts . . .

about being here right now . . .

your unconscious mind has its own thoughts . . .

*and its own ways to **use** these **quiet times** . . .*

sinking within . . .

*to **work** for you now . . .*

***in your own way** . . .*

knowing that no matter what words may be heard . . .

*why your **unconscious mind** . . .*

has the words it needs to hear . . .

*to allow you to **receive** . . .*

what you came here to know . . .

***from yourself** . . .*

and the unconscious mind can now . . . go ahead . . .

and use these words . . .

in the most appropriate and respectful manner for you . . .

A s your unconscious mind continues . . .

*to **search through** that experience . . .*

*that is **your experience now** . . .*

*that experience **that you are** . . .*

***a unique person** . . . an individual self . . .*

allow your unconscious mind . . .

*to **explore** those **new ways** to free you . . .*

to dance with yourself . . .

*in **new patterns** of rhythm and flow . . .*

because sometimes . . .

there are times . . .

*when you might like **to just** slide on down . . .*

*and **rest within yourself** . . .*

free of that need to defend and fight . . .

free of that need to argue and be right . . .

*perhaps there are times when you'd just like **to be** . . .*

***with the sounds** of life . . .*

***with the beauty** as it unfolds . . .*

***the feelings** of wonder **as they come** . . .*

*W*hatever situation . . .

might be a time when you'd like to dance with your self . . .

in yet another way . . .

relaxing . . . resting . . .

*why perhaps your **unconscious mind** can . . .*

*continue to **explore** now . . .*

*new **ways to relate to that sense of self** . . .*

like the waves of the ocean that come and go . . .

each wave . . .

*while it is a wave . . . is **connected** with the sea . . .*

***yet** . . . **separate** in itself as a wave . . .*

and when the wave falls back . . . disappearing into the sea . . .

it loses that form of a wave, does it not? . . .

and the ocean absorbs . . . that wave . . .

welcoming it back . . . inside the depths . . .

yet while the wave was a wave . . .

it was a wave unique in itself . . . isn't it? . . .

free to move with the rhythm of the sea . . .

*and how **substantial** is a wave really? . . .*

as substantial as a rock . . .

feeling so solid to the touch? . . .

a rock so solid that when a person stubs their toe . . .

*why it hurts? . . . and **yet** . . .*

physicists now say . . . there is nothing there . . .

no substance of solidity at all . . .

just those energy currents criss-crossing this way and that . . .

giving the feel of a substance . . .

allowing the feel of solidity . . .

and is the rock . . . really there? . . .

*and of course, your **unconscious***

***mind** can **explore** . . .*

just how it is that a person can . . .

draw many lines on a piece of paper that was blank . . .

criss-crossing those lines like lines of energy . . .

and where many lines cross a point . . .

a point begins to arise . . . that wasn't there before . . .

a point that appears solid . . .

separate from the lines crossing back and forth across the page . . .

and when many lines cross back and forth . . .

why a big point arises, does it not? . . .

a dot . . . right there . . .

and is a point really there? . . . separate from those lines . . .

or is it a part of the motion . . . a part of the movement . . .

the coming to a comfortable place . . .

where the point seems to be . . .

*A*nd it's curious how a person can . . .

look *up to the sky at night . . .*

and out of all those stars so vast and bright . . .

*the eyes can seek and **find** the Big Dipper . . .*

the eyes drawing imaginary lines . . .

connecting those stars twinkling in the skies . . .

until a dipper of enormous size appears . . .

and is a Big Dipper really there . . . in the sky? . . .

*or do the eyes simply **allow that** illusion **to come clear** for*

awhile . . .

*L*ike the images arising from those light rays bending . . .

as they hit the layers of air and differing temperatures . . .

differing densities . . .

creating that mirage . . .

like a shimmering . . . shining . . . image . . .

a vision on the highway ahead . . .

actually an image of the sky . . .

bending its reflections against the air . . .

*and that **illusion is real** . . . **yet** . . .*

*the object . . . is **not there** . . .*

...holding that sparkler and daring ...to write his name...

*H*ow many times . . .

has a child been delighted . . .

by watching the sparkles of a sparkler . . .

celebrating freedom . . .

moving that sparkler round and round . . .

perhaps even holding that pencil of light and daring . . .

to write his name in the air . . .

as the sparkler sparkles . . .

and by the time that child is done . . .

why the name has vanished, hasn't it? . . .

out of sight . . .

and even the first letter of the name . . .

disappears before you can begin the second . . .

Like writing your name in water . . .

by the time you finish . . .

running your finger across the surface of the sea . . .

signing your name in liquid motion . . .

why the signature is no longer there . . . is it? . . .

and when a person . . . takes a lighted torch . . .

whirling it in a circle . . .

allowing an image . . .

of a circle of light to come . . .

so clear, so obvious to the eye . . .

is a circle of light . . . really there? . . .

or is the torch simply moving . . .

from one moment to the next . . .

*in **a pattern** . . .*

*that **allows that image to come, so real** . . .*

yet is a circle . . .

really there . . .

as something separate . . .

from that moving light? . . .

...does the wave that a surfer rides really stand there?...

> *when the waves of the ocean move . . .*
>
> *does the wave that a surfer rides . . .*
>
> *really just stand there . . .*
>
> *allowing the surfer to **use its substance** . . .*
>
> ***as a solid place to stand?** . . .*
>
> *or is that wave . . .*
>
> *seemingly so high and big . . .*
>
> *a force moving fast across the water . . .*
>
> *seemingly the same? . . . yet . . .*
>
> *the waters constantly change . . .*

*A*nd it's curious to know . . .

when a piece of bamboo becomes hollow . . .

why its song can sing . . .

yet *a bamboo can only have the credit . . .*

of not destroying the song . . .

of allowing the song to come through its hollowness inside . . .

allow*ing* **the emptiness there** . . .

*F*or after all the layers . . .

have been removed . . .

from an onion . . .

peeling it off piece by piece . . .

what finally does remain . . . is an **emptiness** . . .

and what is an emptiness but a doorway . . .

is an emptiness . . .

with a fullness . . .

all its own . . .

and what is a doorway . . .

but a nothingness . . .

an invisible, pregnant womb . . .

out of which something can emerge . . .

*A*nd your **unconscious mind** *can* . . .

begin to **know** *its* **own experience** *now* . . .

and **explore** *allowing that experience* . . .

to move with you to **create** . . . **new guidelines** . . .

new ways **to move with that sense of self** . . .

letting **go** *of those* **old beliefs** . . .

decided from your own experience . . .

you're ready to be free of now . . .

and how long does it take a person . . .

to **recognize** *the futility of boxing with the shadows* . . .

like **that reflection** *fighting the robins and the cardinals*

engage in daily . . .

a process relating to defending their territory . . .

why they fight . . .

their very own reflection they see in the windows . . .

that reflection reflecting back in the shinyness of a hub cap . . .

why those little birds fight and box with their own shadow . . .

never seeming to **learn** . . .

there is no bird there . . .

and the robin will return day after day . . .

to take up battle again and again with that reflection . . .

but a mirroring . . . *a bending of the light* . . .

*while **no one is really there** . . :*

and yet that bird feels the solidity of that reflection . . .

of course . . .

everybody knows where there is the solidity of ice . . .

*there is water waiting to **flow again** . . .*

and the frozen solidity of those old ideas . . .

you're ready to become free of now . . .

*why the **unconscious mind** can continue . . .*

*to **melt away** those frozen iceblock **illusions** layer by layer . . .*

***allow**ing the fluidity . . .*

*of your being . . . your self . . . in **new ways** now . . .*

continuing to be created . . .

Because it's curious to know . . .

a material that is a good conductor . . .

is one that has little resistance . . .

*metals **allow** the current to **flow** right on through . . .*

allowing fewer collisions between the electrons flowing . . .

and the very atoms of the conductor itself . . .

and you can allow your **unconscious mind** . . .

to **conduct the creation of these new possibilities** . . .

in your way now . . .

reflecting . . . the uniqueness . . . of your self . . .

allow*ing that* **awareness** . . .

to become even **more available now** . . .

as you explore how it feels . . .

to be like an empty boat . . .

when you choose the time is

right . . .

to **let go** *of that fight* . . .

and **relax** . . .

trust your own

experience *now* . . .

because you are **learn***ing* . . .

you can **be yourself** . . . **comfortably** . . .

and your **unconscious mind** *can* . . .

continue to explore *your experience now* . . .

all . . . **of that experience that is yours to know** . . .

and **use these knowings** *now* . . .

to allow that unconscious mind . . .

to work for you . . . **in new ways** . . .

W*hile that continues on now . . . I wonder if
you're aware . . .
no matter how many knots there are . . .*
in a handkerchief . . .
why that handkerchief still has the same quality . . .
as before those knots were tied up in that cloth . . .
and when the knots were put in . . .
why, of course . . .
the handkerchief became different . . . didn't it? . . .
nothing was really added . . .
and nothing was destroyed . . .
but it was still not quite the same . . .
except when knots are tied in a handkerchief . . .
it is no longer free to be fully itself . . .
open wide . . .

A*nd a handkerchief tied in knots . . .*
becomes a slave to those knots . . .
*and loses its **freedom to open** itself fully . . .*
*and your **unconscious mind** knows . . .*
*it can continue to **untie the knots** . . .*
that you have chosen are the knots that it's time to untie now . . .
***from the past** . . .*

and **come to the present** . . .

that is yours to receive . . . isn't it? . . .

fresh . . .

alive with the new inspiration of each breath you breathe . . .

f course . . .

your unconscious mind will **do this work** . . .

in the **most appropriate manner for you** . . .

continuing to take these learnings with you now . . .

even as you've learned how to **relax,** *didn't you? . . .*

with your experience here . . .

you can **take these learnings with you** . . .

right on outside of this space . . .

right on beyond these words . . .

and allow your unconscious mind to use these learnings . . .

these unnoticed experiences . . .

recognized now and in the future . . .

in the most meaningful manner for you . . .

unique . . . in all the world . . .

*A*llowing . . . *your self* . . .

can continue now . . .

to know . . . what it's time for you to know . . .

you can . . . be yourself . . . comfortably . . .

*and continue to **learn*** . . .

the feel of trusting yourself . . .

and the experience . . . that is yours . . .

and just as you've experienced here . . .

a movement outside of your normal self . . .

outside of your normal mind . . .

outside of your normal way of moving and relating to life . . .

*you can **allow** that **learning** to go with you* . . .

*even as you begin to **gently become aware*** . . .

your energies are continuing to shift now . . .

moving** you **toward that awareness of your self . . .

that is you . . . resting there . . .

in that place where you began this journey here . . .

allowing yourself now to follow these words . . .

like a thread . . . pulling you and calling you more and more . . .

gently and easily now . . . toward this time and place . . .

feeling the energy returning . . .

your awareness coming into that body . . .

even though the cells of that body have changed . . .

died and replaced themselves . . .

hundreds and thousands of times . . .

that body is still sitting right here . . .

right now . . .

feeling the **energies** coming more and **more alive** . . .

into the **body now** . . .

awakening yourself as much as you dare . . .

*to just be **here** . . .*

*awake and alert, **now**.*

wake up!

THOUGHTS:

Epilogue

Annie is gone now. My times with her seem strange to others, so I speak of them rarely. As I stood in her room one last time, I could feel her presence lingering, reaching out beyond the boundaries of the walls and windows, melting inside the wind and the trees and the birds singing their morning song.

I remember her beauty now when the sun's warmth caresses my face, or I notice the morning glory celebrating the dawn of the day. Her words and wisdom have somehow settled in my heart, her presence having transformed my awareness of my Being. Even my mind likes to recall her words, allowing them to echo forward through time, touching and transforming these moments of now. I may even have become a bit more poetic through knowing her.

Of course, she would say my poetry was always here, simply waiting for me to allow it voice, my love always here waiting for me to open my heart, my truth never deserting me, just waiting to be recognized and received. Maybe she was right. If so, perhaps her incredible beauty and grace is also mine, waiting hidden in the beasts still left for me to meet and befriend.

My journey goes on now and the quest for my awareness and courage and trust somehow easier, for I know they are there within me. I find myself relaxing when the darkness comes, when the pain lashes out, when the endings and the loss come to claim their time. Annie was right. They are a part of the fabric of life. Allowing them seems to give me more freedom to enjoy the light, the pleasure, and the new beginnings endlessly arriving again and again.

My mind is somehow more quiet these days, allowing me to experience the sights and sounds, the tastes and smells and feel of life with a little less judgement and comparison. I don't understand this life, but I'm more relaxed now. My heart knows that it is simply a mystery to explore. With Annie's help, I'm more able to let go now, somehow at ease with myself and my journey in a new whole way.

If these remembrances have touched your spirit as Annie touched mine, perhaps you too can relax a little more now as you travel your journey, alone and together, in the darkness and the light. And whether the song of your soul is heard as a lion's roar, or the quiet, fragile whisper of a small flower daring to open, you may find yourself trusting an inner knowing that existence is awaiting your arrival, ready to celebrate your coming home.

Lions In Wait

for
Osho

Appendix

To The Student of Ericksonian Hypnosis and NLP

For students of Ericksonian Hypnosis and NLP, *Lions In Wait* provides excellent examples of Ericksonian Language Patterns, marking, use of truisms, metaphor, and time shifting in a story-telling format.

Lions In Wait demonstrates pacing and leading in the specifically vague style basic to the Ericksonian approach and reflects the ability of this style to maintain respect for the individual process.

The structure of each chapter will be of interest. A problem state is defined in the beginning of each chapter through Nicholas's thoughts and feelings. Since every seeker has some idea of his "goal", how it will feel in sensory experience, how it will change his life, what he would need to get there and what stops him, it would be folly to work with any particular spiritual content.

Facticity is all about the recognition of duality and the re-structuring of the unconscious level of the mind to have choiceless awareness as an option, or the ability to allow certain facticities (Opposites) to exist without aversion or clinging. Many seekers represent their spiritual quests in a way that does not meet the NLP conditions of well-formedness, primarily because it is not possible to get rid of either the dark or the light when resting *inside the mind.* There is no challenge in Facticity to the reality that there is a place where duality no longer resides, but that place cannot be within the realm of the mind/body. All experience when put through the mind automatically takes the dual shape.

So, a well-formed outcome would better include the understanding that what is being sought can only be found outside the mind itself. The totality of these trances is to help the unconscious mind re-shape and restructure its basic understanding of Opposites, based upon what it can know experientially - and when the mind recognizes that the Facticity of Opposites is, in fact, the most basic pattern in our experience of life, it can and does begin to relax and recreate its guidelines and behaviors in new directions.

The arena of resources is already pinpointed in Facticity as our *discounted* experiences, i.e., experiences we have neglected to recognize as valuable, useful and relevant. The blocks to reviewing these experiences and seeing their value are assumed to be certain beliefs and assumptions about our basic relationship to Opposites and our sense of self.

Because our minds are already conditioned to look outside for approval and information before looking inward, these trance-scripts pace and lead the person toward the inside by accepting, amplifying and utilizing basic truisms or undeniably true *discounted* experience most often found first in nature and then the human body. Once enough truisms of this nature have been evoked, the trances move into areas that may not be absolutely within the readers' personal experience, but are known to them and generally accepted as true.

It is important to note that Facticity does not lead anyone to a particular content, but rather leads the individual to explore particular possibilities, perhaps not recognized before. No one should read these trances or engage in Facticity without the desire to move beyond believing into knowing what is knowable about life.

In Chapter One, the outcome is to re-educate the unconscious mind to the inevitability of change and its abilities to relax with that process.

In Chapter Two, the outcome is to alert the unconscious mind to the presence and relevance of the most basic pattern woven in the very fabric of constant change, i.e., the pattern of duality. An additional outcome is to alert the unconscious mind to the recognition that the opposition it sees in duality is, in fact, only one perspective and a complementariness can be perceived from another point of view.

In Chapter Three, the outcome is to expand the unconscious mind's definition and/or understanding of death beyond the projected termination of the physical body causing the end of everything. This is done by offering an exploration of death as an ending which always seems to bring with it a beginning, or the complementariness of life and death. This Chapter also explores discovering values for the usually avoided experiences of pressure and pain, inviting readers to begin to relax their avoidance and approach these undeniable experiences in living with another attitude.

Chapters Four and Five deal with the human dilemma of our need to be connected with each other, and our need to be unique, special and/or alone. They are separate chapters because here is where one of our most basic splits has occurred. Most of us are solidly identified with one or the other as the *right* way to be. Those who have chosen togetherness, usually don't know *experientially* their own uniqueness, or feel at ease in the presence of themselves alone. Those who have chosen aloneness usually don't know *experientially* the validity of connectedness as a human need and a human condition.

These Chapters offer new ways for the unconscious mind to relate to these facticities, answering general objections and concerns. Chapter Four wishes to point out and offer verification that connections do exist and are an integral part of life. Chapter Five wishes to point out that aloneness, from a specific point of view, is a place where uniqueness and specialness can blossom. This is based on the premise that to be unique or special intrinsically means you are an individual and there is no one else like you. Unconscious fear of being alone will often block the individuals from finding themselves. Thus, an expanded perception is offered to the unconscious mind which is generally conditioned to be either for or against these relationship states.

In Chapter Six, the outcome is to offer the re-creation of balance as a major strategy for relaxing with duality. It also includes expanding the unconscious mind's understanding of balance from being a place to reach or attain, to a process which is constantly recreating itself, i.e., balancing in motion.

In Chapter Seven, the outcome is to strengthen the readers trust in their own discounted experience of life, urge the unconscious mind to strengthen the resource states of trust and courage, and explore the possiblity of moving beyond beliefs as the major source of guidelines into the readers discounted experiences and conscious spiritual learning.

In Chapter Eight, the outcome is to evoke the unconscious mind's ability to recognize value in any experience of life. The purpose of this is to create a positive mind without denying or ignoring the darker or unpleasant realities of experiential living. It is known to be much easier to step into mental health and No-Mind from a positive mind than from one that is negative.

In Chapter Nine, the outcome is to shift the unconscious mind from the conditioning that consciousness or awareness, or generally anything of a spiritual nature, must be attained or earned. The possiblity is given that what the seeker is in search of is already here and already his, and that acceptance and relaxation will allow the seeker to fall back inside what is naturally ours to know, i.e., our spiritual dimension. Again, exploration of the reader's own *experience* is suggested and not the installation of a new *belief*.

In Chapter Ten, the outcome is to offer the unconscious mind an alternative perception of the self or the ego so that it can relax with the possiblity of experientially discovering that we are, in fact, a part of the whole, and that the whole is greater than the sum of its parts.

The allegorical format of these trance-scripts trigger the TDS phenomena (the unconscious search for meaning) and utilizes indirect associative focusing, thereby insuring the unconscious mind the freedom to take anything that is useful and appropriate and reject anything that is not.

However, as with all good pieces of work, we should be working for the client's outcome and not our own, and this is why it is important to be aware that Facticity truly is appropriate only for those who *consciously* wish to move beyond believing into knowing what is possible to be known.

The Facticity Experience, a two-week intensive personal exploration, utilizes these skills to re-shape and re-structure the psychology of our own unconscious mind to create choicelessness as a new choice, or the option of Both/And as well as Either/Or (See *Facticity - A Door To Mental Health And Beyond.*).

The recognition of Opposites as a most basic facticity of life *through the mind* is producing amazing results. For students who wish to deepen their understanding of Facticity as an application of NLP and Ericksonian Hypnosis to the acceleration of human consciousness, see *Facticity - A Door To Mental Health & Beyond.*

For information on attending a Facticity Experience, participating in Facticity Trainings NLP/Hypnosis Certification trainings, or purchasing the Ericksonian Hypnosis Tape series *Remembrance* and *Facticity*, please contact:

Facticity Trainings, Inc.
P.O. Box 22814
Seattle, Washington 98122 U.S.A.
(206) 462-4369

Lions In Wait

Bibliography

General References:

Capra, F. *The Tao Of Physics*, Berkeley, CA: Shambhala Press, 1975.

Daumal, Rene *Mount Analogue*, CA: Shambhala Press, 1981.

Goldstein, Joseph *The Experience of Insight*, Santa Cruz, CA: Unity Press, 1976.

Kornfield, Jack *Living Buddhist Masters*, Santa Cruz, CA: Unity Press, 1977.

Krishnamurti, J. *Freedom From The Known*, San Francisco, CA: Harper, 1969.

Krishnamurti, J. *Meditations*, India: Krishnamurti Foundation, 1979.

Levine, S. *A Gradual Awakening*, New York: Anchor Books, 1979.

Merrell-Wolff, F. *The Philosophy of Consciousness Without An Object*, New York: The Julian Press, 1973.

Merton, Thomas *The Way of Chuang Tzu*, New York: New Directions, 1965.

Michaels, R.E. *Facticity - A Door To Mental Health And Beyond*, Seattle, WA: Facticity Trainings, Inc., 1992.

Michaels, R.E. *Storytelling The Truth*, (pending final publication 1995).

Osho, *Hidden Harmony (on Heraclitus)*, India: Rajneesh Foundation, 1976.

Osho, *When The Shoe Fits (on Chuang Tzu)*, India: Rajneesh Foundation, 1977.

Osho, *Neither This Nor That (on 3rd Zen Patriarch)*, India: Rajneesh Foundation, 1975.

Reps, Paul *Zen Flesh, Zen Bones*, New York: Anchor Books, Doubleday, 1933.

Sujata, A. *Beginning to See*, Santa Cruz, CA: Unity Press, 1975.

Suzuki, S. *Zen Mind, Beginner's Mind*, New York: Weatherhill, Inc., 1970.

NLP and Ericksonian References:

Andreas, C. & S. *The Heart Of The Mind*, Utah: Real People Press, 1989.

Bandler, R. *Use Your Brain For A Change*, Utah: Real People Press, 1985.

Bandler, R. & Grinder, J. *The Structure of Magic, I & II*, Palo Alto, CA: Science and Behavior Books, 1975.

Bandler, R. & Grinder, J. *Patterns I*, Cupertino, CA: Meta Publications, 1975.

Bandler, R. & Grinder, J. *Tranceformations*, Utah: Real People Press, 1981.

Dilts R. *Changing Beliefs with NLP,* Cupertino, CA: Meta
Publications, 1990.

Erickson, Milton H. *Healing In Hypnosis,* New York: Irvington
Publishers, 1983.

Erickson, Milton H. & Edited by Rossi, Ernest L. *The Collected
Papers of Milton H. Erickson on Hypnosis, Vol. 1-1V,* New
York: Irvington Publishers, 1980.

James, Tad, *Time Line Therapy and The Basis of Personality,*
Cupertino, California: Meta Publications, 1988.

Lewis, B. & Pucelik, F. *Magic Demystified,* Lake Oswego, OR:
Metamorphous Press, 1982.

O'Hanlon, W. H. *Tap Roots,* New York: Norton & Co., 1987.

Ornstein, R. Ph.D. & Sobel, D. M.D. *The Healing Brain,* New
York: Simon & Schuster, 1987.

Rossi, Ernest L. & Erickson, Milton H., *Hypnotic Realities,* New
York: Irvington Publishers, 1976.

About The Author

Ragini Elizabeth Michaels has been working with people as a Clinical Hypnotherapist and a Trainer of NLP and Ericksonian Hypnosis for over eighteen years. She travels worldwide presenting Facticity to a wide variety of audiences.

As the author of six critically acclaimed audio tapes and the creator of the Facticity Process (a group experience), Ragini relishes in continuing the exploration of new and creative applications of NLP and Hypnosis to the advancement of human consciousness.

Lions In Wait is the follow-up to Ragini's first book *Facticity - A Door To Mental Health And Beyond.* Ragini lives in the Pacific Northwest and enjoys her leisure time walking, playing music and drawing.

Facticity Trainings, Inc.

Facticity Trainings is dedicated to the support and advancement of human consciousness in the fields of communication and behavioral change. Our commitment to evoking conscious awareness, as well as excellence and elegance in the training and performance of Practitioners of NLP and Hypnosis, creates training programs high in quality, self-awareness and heart.

Facticity Trainings recognizes that a *better* mind may not be of much value unless non-judgemental awareness and new levels of consciousness are available to guide that mind in the service of the human heart and spirit.

Facticity Trainings offers Certification programs at the Practitioner and Master Practitioner levels of NLP. These programs provide concurrent training in Ericksonian Hypnosis and Facticity.

Facticity Trainings is the publisher of Ms. Michaels' two critically acclaimed Ericksonian Hypnosis audio tape series, *Remembrance* and *Facticity*, as well as her first book, *Facticity - A Door To Mental Health And Beyond*, and her new book to be released in 1995 - *Storytelling The Truth*.

Facticity Trainings Audio

featuring Acoustic Associative Hypnosis (AAH)

Each tape offers one side with a trance accompanied by original music and the other side with just the music alone. Both the *Facticity Series* and *Remembrance Series* tapes take the idea of subliminal hypnosis one step further.

Subliminal tapes provide a voice outside the individual telling the person what to do. Acoustic Associative Hypnosis (AAH) evokes your unconscious ability to create by itself the words you need to hear, the images you need to see, and the feelings you want to feel.

After listening to the trance side just a few times, your unconscious will associate the words, and the inner experience they create, with the music. Listening to just the music side will cause your unconscious mind to remember the words and continue utilizing them in the most appropriate way for you.

The dance between Ragini's soothing and melodious voice and Ambodha's inspired and transforming music carries you spaciously and graciously toward whatever depths or heights you're ready to explore.

Facticity tapes utilize Digital Stereo Processing in addition to extended frequency response. Orignial music is composed, performed, and recorded by Divyam Ambodha. All music has been crafted to work in concert with the theme of each tape.

Trance-Scripts

Each audio tape in the *Facticity Series* and *Remembrance Series* has been transcribed for those interested in learning the underlying Ericksonian linguistic patterns. These patterns are often referred to as Milton Model Language Patterns and are clearly notated on each transcription. There is one trance-script for each of the six tapes.

Facticity Series

Beginning & Endings - relaxing with change - works to re-educate your unconscious mind to the presence of change and its hidden pattern of flow from one extreme toward its seeming opposite and back again. A relaxing and soothing reminder that change is natural and you can learn to relax with this flow.

Balancing In Motion - works to strengthen your unconscious mind's awareness that balance is a process, rather than a position to achieve, freeing you to more easily experience that balancing in motion.

Remembrance Series

Answers Rest Within - provides a beautiful and relaxing way to re-educate your unconscious mind to look within for the answers you seek.

Awareness Arising - supports the ability of your unconscious mind to heighten your awareness and allow you to be in the moment - here and now.

Beyond The Past - guides your unconscious mind in how to let go of what is no longer needed, keeping the learnings and freeing you to move beyond those conditions of long ago.

Healing Heart - works to heal wounds of the heart and evoke the heart's capacity to forgive, to accept and to allow the love to flow.

Lions In Wait

Facticity Books

Facticity - A Door To Mental Health And Beyond offers a new avenue of exploration for *how* to relax with both the light and dark aspects of our human nature. This book reveals the results of a ten year study that looked into the success and difficulties of those seeking to define their identity from a spiritual perspective. It offers a new model for movement beyond the mind utilizing NLP and Ericksonian Hypnosis and offers insights into the need for shifting our experience of living from the conflict that arises from an *either/or* perspective toward the acceptance and balance that emerges when a *both/and* point of view is allowed.

Lions In Wait - a road to personal courage demonstrates the heart of Facticity via trance-scripts given spontaneously in 1987. A delightful book of truisms presented in an allegorical format utilizing all the elements of the Ericksonian Hypnotic style. *Lions* chronicals the inner journey of Nicholas and his interaction with Annie, a hypnotic storyteller who always leads him back to himself. An excellent book for practitioners of NLP, Hypnosis and all kinds of therapy.

Storytelling The Truth is a compilation of over 400 truisms and metaphors relating to the re-education of the unconscious mind toward duality. This includes many beautiful examples of hypnotic storytelling at its best. Pending publication in 1995.

Facticity Reviews

"Thank you for the gift of Facticity. You have made it easy to understand how the mind and the emotions can be integrated with the spiritual sense we are all seeking . . . . Your book is the only NLP book I've read that easily and successfully blends together the notions of self (body, mind and spirit) . . . . "

Tim Loebs, M.A., South Carolina
Psychotherapist

" I still use what I learned from reading Facticity - A Door To Mental Health And Beyond and share the concepts with clients and students. There is no higher complement I could give a book. Facticity is a refreshing synthesis of NLP technology and consciousness exploration which results in the best of both."

Steve David, Ph.D.
Manitoba, Canada
Director of Training & Therapy

"Whatever can help people to not take this illusion of opposites seriously is helpful since Truth can dawn only on a quiet mind. In my opinion, your book is most useful for this. The pictures are wonderful and I'm sure many people will enjoy this book!"

Ingrid Saur, Connecticut
Counselor

"Thanks for an excellent book! The recognizing of opposites and owning their importance in our lives deserves the consideration of any serious student. The quotes, the prose and the poetry for the unconscious mind - Excellent!"

Clinton Clay, LCSW
Mid-South Institute of NLP

"Facticity is very well written. Neither the concepts of NLP nor embracing opposites are new to me, but the ways in which they are integrated continually provided new insights and perspectives. This is a book I could easily recommend to clients who are ready to embrace a larger perspective."

Sylvia Runkle, Illinois
Counselor & NLP Practitioner

"I found the trance phrases to be quite delightful as an interrupt through the left-headed process. I read the book in one sitting and felt more integrated and more 'oneness' at the end of the book."

V. Jan Marszalek, President
Learning Systems Corporation

"Facticity is beautifully done and filled with meditations and suggestions I'm sure will be helpful to practitioners and counselors and general readers. After reading your book, I am left with great respect for your work and its deep and spiritual integration."

Jack Kornfield, Ph.D.
Psychologist & Author of
Seeking the Heart of Wisdom

"I have never read an NLP book that speaks to both my conscious and unconscious mind simultaneously, doing what it is speaking about even as I read. A most unique approach guiding us beyond paradox into a personal re-discovering of our spiritual dimension beyond the mind. Fascinating and good reading."

Joseph Vidmar, Ph.D.
Psychologist & NLP Trainer

"*Finally, a book of hypnosis and NLP which explores the area beyond mind. With clarity and in a simple readable way, Ragini takes the reader on a journey into expanded consciousness, daring to approach the space of no-mind, meditation or witnessing. An important book for exploring the interface between the psychological and spiritual dimensions of life.*"

Dharma Books
Germany

"*The most interesting synthesis of psychotherapy and meditation I have read in a long while. Inductions placed beautifully in the text lead the reader from the realm of duality into the present moment. A very innovative and worthwhile book.*"

Prof. Charles Fisher
Brandeis University

Tape Reviews

"*I would recommend these tapes to any of my students . . . Ragini Michaels has excellent control of the subtleties of this art.*"

Nancy L. Beplat
Rapporter

"*Ragini's tapes certainly are fine examples of Ericksonian trance induction techniques and allowed me to quickly and easily drift into a relaxed, calm state.*"

Will MacDonald, NLP Northwest
An Insiders Guide to Sub-Modalities

"*The Facticity tapes have the best music in terms of composition and follow the (Ericksonian) style with the most creative use of language.*"

Sandy LaForge
Anchor Point

Order Form – Tapes

Tape   Trance-Script
Qty.   Qty.

_____ _____ Beginnings & Endings

_____ _____ Balancing In Motion

_____ _____ Answers Rest Within

_____ _____ Awareness Arising

_____ _____ Beyond The Past

_____ _____ Healing Heart

_____ _____ **Total(s)**

        _____ Tape Price (see below)

        _____ Trance-Script Price (see below)

        _____ Shipping & Handling (see next page)

        _____ Washington Residents add 8.2%

        _____ **TOTAL** Enclosed for Tapes and
Trance-Scripts

Tape Prices
1 tape $14.95—2 tapes $26.95—3 tapes $39.95—4 tapes $49.95
5 or more tapes $11.95 Each

Trance-Script Prices
1-3 Trance-Scripts $4.95 Each—4 or More $3.95 Each

Order Form – Books

_____	Copies of *Facticity* @ $16.95	=	_____
_____	Copies of *Lions in Wait* @ $16.95	=	_____
	Shipping & Handling (see below)	=	_____
	Washington Residents add 8.2%	=	_____
	TOTAL	=	_____

Shipping & Handling - 1st Class/Air

Tapes/Domestic	$1.50 1st Tape, $.50 Each Additional Tape
Tapes/International	$3.00 1st Tape, $1.00 Each Additional Tape
Books/Domestic	$3.75
Books/International	$7.50
Trance-Scripts	$1.00 Domestic $2.50 International

International Orders

Must be American Express International Money Order or check drawn on banks with a branch in the U.S.A. Monies must be in US funds only.

Please send information on NLP and Hypnosis Trainings

Please send information on The Facticity Experience

Please send information on audio version of *Lions in Wait*

Name _____

Address Apt. # _____

City State Country Zip _____

Day Phone Evening Phone _____

Mail Your Payment to: **Facticity Trainings, Inc., Post Office Box 22814, Seattle, WA 98122, U.S.A. Phone 206-462-4369**